AUTO-BIOGRAPHY

This page enables you to compile a list of useful data on your car, so that whether you're ordering spares or just checking the tyre pressures, all the key information - the information that is 'personal' to your car - is easily within reach.

Registration number: ....

Model: ....

Body colour: ....

Paint code number: ....

Date of first registration: ....

Date of manufacture (if different): ....

VIN (or 'chassis') number: ....

Engine number: ....

Ignition key number: ....

Door lock key/s number/s: ....

Fuel locking cap key number (if fitted): ....

Alarm remote code (if fitted): ....

Alarm remote battery type: ....

Radio/cassette security code (if fitted): ....

Tyre size

Front: ....Rear: ....

Tyre pressure (normally laden)

Front: ....Rear: ....

Tyre pressure (fully laden)

Front: ....Rear: ....

Insurance

    Name and address of insurer:...

    ....

    Policy number:...

Modifications

    Information that might be useful when you need to purchase parts:...

    ....

Suppliers

    Address and telephone number of your garage and parts suppliers:

    ....

    ....

First published in 1996 by Porter Publishing Ltd.

Porter Publishing Ltd.
The Storehouse
Little Hereford Street
Bromyard
Hereford HR7 4DE
England

© Copyright Lindsay Porter and Porter Publishing Ltd, 1996.

British Library Cataloguing in Publication Data.

A catalogue record for this book is available from the British Library.

ISBN 1-899238-17-4

Series Editor: Lindsay Porter
Design: Martin Driscoll, Lindsay Porter and Lyndsay Berryman
Layout and Typesetting: Pineapple Publishing, Worcester
Cover photography: Jeremy Gale
Printed in England by The Trinity Press, Worcester.

Every care has been taken to ensure that the material contained in this Service Guide is correct. However, no liability can be accepted by the authors or publishers for damage, loss, accidents, or injury resulting from any omissions or errors in the information given.

Copyright in all line drawings supplied by The Peugeot Talbot Motor Co Plc remains the property of The Peugeot Talbot Motor Co Plc.

Titles in this Series:
Absolute Beginners' Service Guide
Auto Electrics - DIY Service Manual
Caravan Owner's Manual & Service Guide
Classic 'Bike Service Guide
Diesel Car Engines Service Guide
Ford Escort (Front Wheel Drive) & Orion Service Guide
Ford Fiesta (All models to 1995) Service Guide
Ford Sierra (All models) Service Guide
Land Rover Series I, II, III Service Guide
Land Rover Discovery & Range Rover Service Guide
Land Rover Defender, 90 & 110 Service Guide
Metro (1980-1990) Service Guide
MG Midget & Austin-Healey Sprite Service Guide
Mini (all models 1959-1994) Service Guide
MGB (including MGC, MGB GT V8 and MG RV8) Service Guide
Peugeot 205 Service Guide
Vauxhall Astra & Belmont (All models-1995) Service Guide
Vauxhall Cavalier Service Guide
Vauxhall Nova Service Guide
VW Beetle Service Guide

- With more titles in production -

Peugeot 205

Service Guide
& Owner's Manual

by
Andrew MacQuillan
& Lindsay Porter

OIL AND WATER DON'T MIX

It is important to remember that even a small quantity of oil is harmful to water and wildlife. And tipping oil down the drain is as good as tipping it into a river. Many drains are connected directly to a river or stream and pollution will occur.

Each year the National Rivers Authority deals with over 6,000 oil related water pollution incidents. Many of these are caused by the careless disposal of used oil.

OIL POLLUTES WATER
USE YOUR BRAIN-
NOT THE DRAIN!

The used oil from the sump of just one car can cover an area of water the size of two football pitches, cutting off the oxygen supply and harming swans, ducks, fish and other river life.

Follow the Oil Care Code

◆ *When you drain your engine oil - don't oil the drain!* Pouring oil down the drain will cause pollution. It is also an offence.

◆ Don't mix used oil with other materials, such as paint or solvents, because this makes recycling very difficult.

◆ Take used oil to an oil recycling bank. Telephone FREE on 0800 663366 to find the location of your nearest oil bank, or contact your local authority recycling officer.

OIL CARE
FOLLOW THE CODE

This book is produced in association with Castrol (U.K.) Ltd.

"Cars have become more and more sophistated. But changing the oil and brake fluid, and similar jobs are as simple as they ever were. Castrol are pleased to be associated with this book because it gives us the opportunity to make life simpler for those who wish to service their own cars. Castrol have succeeded in making oil friendlier and kinder to the environment by removing harmful chlorine from our range of engine lubricants which in turn prolong the life of the catalytic convertor (when fitted), by noticeably maintaining the engine at peak efficiency. In return, we ask you to be kinder to the environment too... by taking your used oil to your Local Authority Amenity Oil Bank. It can then be used as a heating fuel. Please do not poison it with thinners, paint, creosote or brake fluid because these render it useless and costly to dispose of."

Castrol (U.K.) Ltd

CONTENTS

Introduction

Over the years, I have run any number of cars, from superb classic cars and modern cars, to those with one foot in the breakers yard. And I know only too well that any car is only enjoyable to own if it's safe, reliable and basically sound - and the only way of ensuring that it stays that way is to service it regularly. That's why we have set about creating this book, which aims to show the owner interested in DIY car servicing that there's nothing to fear; you really can do it yourself!

Making It Easy! Porter Publishing Service Guides are the first books to give you all the service information you might need, with step-by-step instructions, along with a complete Service History section for you to complete and fill in as you carry out regular maintenance on your car over the months ahead. Using the information contained in this book, you will be able to:

◆ see for yourself how to carry out every Service Job, from weekly and monthly checks, right up to longer-term maintenance items.
◆ carry out regular body maintenance and rustproofing, saving a fortune in body repairs over the years to come.
◆ enhance the value of your car by completing a full Service History of every maintenance job you carry out on your car.

I hope you enjoy keeping your car in trim while saving lots of money by servicing your car yourself, with the help of this book. Happy motoring!

Lindsay Porter
Porter Publishing Ltd

Lindsay Porter

Andy MacQuillan

Acknowledgements

The Peugeot 205 has been a very successful design in all forms, from economical 'school-and-shopping' runabout, to long-legged diesel-engined motorway cruiser, to the almost frighteningly fast 1.9 GTi. It's a great car and I've enjoyed working on, and finding out about, the model in all its configurations.

I really must thank the staff at Peugeot UK Headquarters for the great assistance they supplied in compiling this book; their help and patience is very much appreciated. However, helpful staff aren't just confined to Peugeot HQ, they're to be found in Peugeot dealerships like Castles Ltd of Leicester, whose staff at Narborough Road branch went beyond the normal call of duty on many occasions, in supplying donor cars and workshop space to photograph them.

Special thanks are due to Portia Dolby, who so very trustingly lent her car to me, a virtual stranger, for many of the photos used here - were it not for the fact she knows my wife, I could've flattered myself into thinking I had a trust-worthy face. Oh well!

Mention of 'the better half' leads me on to thanking the most important person of all - my wife Adele, who made it all possible and, in the end, worthwhile.

Andy MacQuillan

SPECIAL THANKS
The Publisher would like to thank: Peugeot Talbot Motor Co. for their advice and use of illustrative material - Gunsons for equipment, line drawings and advice - Dinitrol for their kind assistance with Chapter 5 - Castrol UK Ltd for lubricants and advice.

CHAPTER 1 - SAFETY FIRST!

You must always ensure that safety is the first consideration in any job you carry out. A slight lack of concentration, or a rush to finish the job quickly can easily result in an accident, as can failure to follow the precautions outlined in this Chapter. Whereas skilled motor mechanics are trained in safe working practices you, the home mechanic, must find them out for yourself and act upon them.

Remember, accidents don't just happen, they are caused, and some of those causes are contained in the following list. Above all, ensure that whenever you work on your car you adopt a safety-minded approach at all times, and remain aware of the dangers that might be encountered.

Be sure to consult the suppliers of any materials and equipment you may use, and to obtain and read carefully any operating and health and safety instructions that may be available on packaging or from manufacturers and suppliers.

PART I: IMPORTANT POINTS

Vehicle Off Ground

ALWAYS ensure that the vehicle is properly supported when raised off the ground. Don't work on, around, or underneath a raised vehicle unless axle stands are positioned under secure, load bearing underbody areas, or the vehicle is driven onto ramps, with the wheels remaining on the ground securely chocked to prevent movement.

ALWAYS ensure that the safe working load rating of any jacks, hoists or lifting gear used is sufficient for the job, and that lifting gear is used only as recommended by the manu-facturer.

NEVER attempt to loosen or tighten nuts that require a lot of force to turn (e.g. a tight oil drain plug) with the vehicle raised, unless it is safely supported. Take care not to pull the vehicle off its supports when applying force to a spanner. Wherever possible, initially slacken tight fastenings before raising the car off the ground.

ALWAYS wear eye protection when working under the vehicle and when using power tools.

Working On The Vehicle

ALWAYS seek specialist advice unless you are justifiably confident about carrying out each job. The safety of your vehicle affects you, your passengers and other road users.

DON'T lean over, or work on, a running engine unless it is strictly necessary, and keep long hair and loose clothing well out of the way of moving mechanical parts. Note that it is theoretically possible for fluorescent striplighting to make an engine fan appear to be stationary - double check whether it is spinning or not! This is the sort of error that happens when you're really tired and not thinking straight. So...

...DON'T work on your car when you're over tired.

ALWAYS work in a well ventilated area and don't inhale dust - it may contain asbestos or other harmful substances.

REMOVE your wrist watch, rings and all other jewellery before doing any work on the vehicle - and especially when working on the electrical system.

DON'T remove the radiator or expansion tank filler cap when the cooling system is hot, or you may get scalded by escaping coolant or steam. Let the system cool down first and even then, if the engine is not completely cold, cover the cap with a cloth and gradually release the pressure.

NEVER drain oil, coolant or automatic transmission fluid when the engine is hot. Allow time for it to cool sufficiently to avoid scalding you.

ALWAYS keep antifreeze, brake and clutch fluid away from vehicle paintwork. Wash off any spills immediately.

TAKE CARE to avoid touching any engine or exhaust system component unless it is cool enough not to burn you.

Running The Vehicle

NEVER start the engine unless the gearbox is in neutral (or 'Park' in the case of automatic transmission) and the hand brake is fully applied.

NEVER run catalytic converter equipped vehicles without the exhaust system heat shields in place.

TAKE CARE when parking vehicles fitted with catalytic

converters. The 'cat' reaches extremely high temperatures and any combustible materials under the car, such as long dry grass, could be ignited.

Personal Safety

NEVER siphon fuel, antifreeze, brake fluid or other such toxic liquids by mouth, or allow contact with your skin. There is an increasing awareness that they can damage your health. Best of all, use a suitable hand pump and wear gloves.

BEFORE undertaking dirty jobs, use a barrier cream on your hands as a protection against infection. Preferably, wear thin gloves, available from DIY outlets.

WEAR GLOVES for sure when there is a risk of used engine oil coming into contact with your skin. It can cause cancer.

WIPE UP any spilt oil, grease or water off the floor immediately, before there is an accident.

MAKE SURE that spanners and all other tools are the right size for the job and are not likely to slip. Never try to 'double-up' spanners to gain more leverage.

SEEK HELP if you need to lift something heavy which may be beyond your capability. Don't forget that when lifting a heavy weight, you should keep your back straight and bend your knees to avoid injuring your back.

NEVER take risky short-cuts or rush to finish a job. Plan ahead and allow plenty of time.

BE METICULOUS and keep the work area tidy - you'll avoid frustration, work better and lose less.

KEEP children and animals right-away from the work area and from unattended vehicles.

ALWAYS tell someone what you're doing and have them regularly check that all is well, especially when working alone on, or under, the vehicle.

PART II: HAZARDS

Fire!

Petrol (gasoline) is a dangerous and highly flammable liquid requiring special precautions. When working on the fuel system, disconnect the vehicle battery earth (ground) terminal whenever possible and always work outside, or in a very well ventilated area. Any form of spark, such as that caused by an electrical fault, by two metal surfaces striking against each other, by a central heating boiler in the garage 'firing up', or even by static electricity built up in your clothing can, in a confined space, ignite petrol vapour causing an explosion. Take great care not to spill petrol on to the engine or exhaust system, never allow any naked flame anywhere near the work area and, above all, don't smoke.

Invest in a workshop-sized fire extinguisher. Choose the carbon dioxide type or preferably, dry powder but never a water type extinguisher for workshop use. Water conducts electricity and can make worse an oil or petrol-based fire, in certain circumstances.

DON'T disconnect any fuel pipes on a fuel injected engine while the ignition is switched on. The fuel in the line is under very high pressure - sufficient to cause serious injury. Remember that many injection systems have residual pressure in the pipes for days after switching off. Consult the workshop manual or seek specialist advice before carrying out any work.

Fumes

In addition to the fire dangers described previously, petrol (gasoline) vapour and the types of vapour given off by many solvents, thinners, and adhesives are highly toxic and under certain conditions can lead to unconsciousness or even death, if inhaled. The

risks are increased if such fluids are used in a confined space so always ensure adequate ventilation when handling materials of this nature. Treat all such substances with care, always read the instructions and follow them with care.

Always ensure that the car is out of doors and not in an enclosed space when the engine is running. Exhaust fumes contain poisonous carbon monoxide, even when the car is fitted with a catalytic converter, since 'cats' sometimes fail and don't function when the engine is cold.

Never drain petrol (gasoline) or use solvents, thinners adhesives or other toxic substances in an inspection pit as the extremely confined space allows the highly toxic fumes to concentrate. Running the engine with the vehicle over the pit can have the same results. It is also dangerous to park a vehicle for any length of time over an inspection pit. The fumes from even a slight fuel leak can cause an explosion when the engine is started. Petrol fumes are heavier than air and will accumulate in the pit.

Mains Electricity

Best of all, avoid the use of mains electricity when working on the vehicle, whenever possible. For instance, you could use rechargeable

tools and a DC inspection lamp, powered from a remote 12V battery - both are much safer. However, if you do use mains-powered equipment, ensure that the appliance is wired correctly to its plug, that where necessary it is properly earthed (grounded), and that the fuse is of the correct rating for the appliance is fitted. For instance, a 13 amp fuse in lead lamp's plug will not provide adequate protection. Do not use any mains powered equipment in damp conditions or in the vicinity of fuel, fuel vapour or the vehicle battery.

Also, before using any mains powered electrical equipment, take one more simple precaution - use an RCD (Residual Current Device) circuit breaker. Then, if there is a short, the RCD circuit breaker minimises the risk of electrocution by instantly cutting the power supply. Buy one from any electrical store or DIY centre. RCDs fit simply into your electrical socket before plugging in your electrical equipment.

The Ignition System

You should never work on the ignition system with the ignition switched on, or with the engine being turned over on the starter, or running.

Touching certain parts of the ignition system, such as the HT leads, distributor cap, ignition coil etc, can result in a severe electric shock. This is especially likely where the insulation on any of these components is weak, or if the components are dirty or damp. Note also that voltages produced by electronic ignition systems are much higher than those produced by conventional systems and could prove fatal, particularly to people with cardiac pacemaker implants. Consult your handbook or main dealer if in any doubt.

An additional risk of injury can arise while working on running engines, if the operator touches a high voltage lead and pulls his or her hand away on to a sharp, conductive or revolving part.

The Battery

Never cause a spark, smoke, or allow a naked light near the vehicle's battery, even in a well ventilated area. Highly explosive hydrogen gas will be given off as part of the charging process.

Battery terminals on the car should be shielded, since a battery contains energy and a spark can be caused by any metal object which touches the battery's terminals or connecting straps.

Before working on the fuel or electrical systems, always disconnect the battery earth (ground) terminal. (But before doing so, read the relevant **FACT FILE** in *Chapter 3* regarding saving computer and radio settings.)

When using a battery charger, care should be taken to avoid causing a spark by switching off the power supply before the battery charger leads are connected or disconnected. Before charging the battery from an external source, disconnect both battery leads before connecting the charger. If the battery is not of the 'sealed-for-life' type, loosen the filler plugs or remove the cover before charging. For best results the battery should be given a low rate trickle charge overnight. Do not charge at an excessive rate or the battery may burst.

Always wear gloves and goggles when carrying or when topping up the battery. Even in diluted form (as it is in the battery) the acid electrolyte is extremely corrosive and must not be allowed to contact the eyes, skin or clothes.

Brakes and Asbestos

Obviously, a car's brakes are among its most important safety related items. ONLY work on your vehicle's braking system if you are trained and competent to do so. If you have not been trained in this work, but wish to carry out the jobs described in this book, we strongly recommend that you have a garage or qualified mechanic check your work before using the car.

Whenever you work on the braking system's mechanical components, or remove front or rear brake pads or shoes: i) wear an efficient particle mask; ii) wipe off all brake dust from the brakes after spraying on a proprietary brand of brake cleaner (never blow dust off with compressed air); iii) dispose of brake dust and discarded shoes or pads in a sealed plastic bag; iv) wash your hands thoroughly after you have finished working on the brakes and certainly before you eat or smoke; v) replace shoes and pads only with asbestos-free shoes or pads. Note that asbestos brake dust can cause cancer if inhaled.

Brake Fluid

Brake fluid absorbs moisture rapidly from the air and can become dangerous resulting in brake failure. Castrol (U.K.) Ltd. recommend that you should have your brake fluid tested at least once a year by a properly equipped garage with test equipment and you should change the fluid in accordance with your vehicle manufacturer's recommendations or as advised in this book if we recommend a shorter interval than the manufacturer. You should buy no more brake fluid than you need, in smaller rather than larger containers. Never store an opened container of brake fluid. Dispose of the remainder at your Local Authority Waste Disposal Site, in the designated disposal unit, not with general waste or with waste oil.

Engine Oils

Take care to observe the following precautions when working with used engine oil. Apart from the obvious risk of scalding when draining the oil from a hot engine, there is the danger from contamination contained in all used oil.

Always wear disposable plastic or rubber gloves when draining the oil from your engine. i) Note that the drain plug and the oil are often hotter than you expect. Wear gloves if the plug is too hot to touch and keep your hand to one side so that you are not scalded by the spurt of oil as the plug comes away; ii) There are very real health hazards associated with used engine oil. In the words of one manufacturer's handbook "Prolonged and repeated contact may cause serious skin disorders, including dermatitis and cancer." Use a barrier cream on your hands and try not to get oil on them. Always wear gloves and wash your hands with hand cleaner soon after carrying out the work. Keep oil out of the reach of children; iii) NEVER, EVER dispose of old engine oil into the ground or down a drain. In the UK, and in most EC countries, every local authority must provide a safe means of oil disposal. In the UK, try your local Environmental Health Department for advice on waste disposal facilities.

Plastic Materials

Work with plastic materials brings additional hazards into workshops. Many of the materials used (polymers, resins, adhesives and materials acting as catalysts and accelerators) contain dangers in the form of poisonous fumes, skin irritants, and the risk of fire and explosions. Do not allow resin or 2-pack adhesive hardener, or that supplied with filler or 2-pack stopper, to come into contact with skin or eyes. Read carefully the safety notes supplied on the can, tube or packaging and always wear impervious gloves and goggles when working with them.

Jacks and Axle Stands

Throughout this book you will see many references to the correct use of jacks, axle stands and similar equipment - and we make

SAFETY FIRST!

no apologies for being repetitive. This is one area where safety cannot be overstressed - your life could be at stake!

Special care must be taken when any type of lifting equipment is used. Jacks are made for lifting the vehicle only, not for supporting it while it is being worked on. Never work under the car using only a jack to support the weight. Jacks must be supplemented by adequate additional means of support, positioned under secure load-bearing parts of the frame or underbody. Axle stands are available from most auto. parts stores. Drive-on ramps are limiting because of their design and size but they are simple to use, reliable and offer the most stable type of support. We strongly recommend their use.

Full details on jacking and supporting the vehicle will be found near the beginning of *Chapter 3*.

Fluoroelastomers
MOST IMPORTANT! PLEASE READ THIS SECTION!

If you service your car in the normal way, none of the following may be relevant to you. Unless, for example, you encounter a car which has been on fire (even in a localised area), subject to heat in, say, a crash-damage repairer's workshop or a vehicle breaker's yard, or if any second-hand parts have been heated in any way.

Many synthetic, rubber-like materials used in motor cars contain a substance called fluorine. These materials are known as fluoroelastomers and are commonly used for oil seals, wiring and cabling, bearing surfaces, gaskets, diaphragms, hoses and 'O' rings. If they are subjected to temperatures greater than 315 degrees C, they will decompose and can be potentially hazardous. Fluoroelastomer materials will show physical signs of

decomposition under such conditions in the form of charring of black sticky masses. Some decomposition may occur at temperatures above 200 degrees C, and it is obvious that when a car has been in a fire or has been dismantled with the assistance of a cutting torch or blow torch, the fluoroelastomers can decompose in the manner indicated above.

In the presence of any water or humidity, including atmospheric moisture, the by-products caused by the fluoroelastomers being heated can be extremely dangerous. According to the Health and Safety Executive, "Skin contact with this liquid or decomposition residues can cause painful and penetrating burns. Permanent irreversible skin and tissue damage can occur". Damage can also be caused to eyes or by the inhalation of fumes created as fluoroelastomers are burned or heated.

After a vehicle has been exposed to fire or high temperatures:

1. Do not touch blackened or charred seals or equipment.

2. Allow all burnt or decomposed fluoroelastomer materials to cool before inspection, investigations, tear-down or removal.

3. Preferably, don't handle parts containing decomposed fluoroelastomers, but if you must, wear goggles and PVC (polyvinyl chloride) or neoprene protective gloves whilst doing so. Never handle such parts unless they are completely cool.

4. Contaminated parts, residues, materials and clothing, including protective clothing and gloves, should be disposed of by an approved contractor to landfill or by incineration according to national or local regulations. Oil seals, gaskets and 'O' rings, along with contaminated material, must not be burned.

PART III: GENERAL WORKSHOP SAFETY

1. Always have a fire extinguisher of the correct type at arm's length when working on the fuel system.

If you do have a fire, DON'T PANIC. Use the extinguisher effectively by directing it at the base of the fire.

2. NEVER use a naked flame anywhere in the workplace.

3. KEEP your inspection lamp well away from any source of petrol (gasoline) such as when disconnecting a carburettor float bowl or fuel line.

4. NEVER use petrol (gasoline) to clean parts. Use paraffin (kerosene), white spirits, or a proprietary degreaser.

5. NO SMOKING. There's a risk of fire or of transferring dangerous substances to your mouth and, in any case, ash falling into mechanical components is to be avoided.

6. BE METHODICAL in everything you do, use common sense, and think of safety at all times.

CHAPTER 2 - BUYING GUIDE

In this Chapter, we show you how to go about buying a second hand car. We also look at which parts wear out, and we explain when they are likely to need replacement, so that whether you are giving your own car the once-over, or you're looking at a prospective purchase, you'll know what to expect; and we examine the best ways of buying parts for your pride and joy.

PART I: BUYING A SECOND-HAND CAR

In general, the safest - but also the most expensive - way of buying second hand is through a main dealer: NOT the same as a general second-hand dealer, whose standards are almost certain to be lower! We *strongly* recommend the use of HPI Autodata checks mentioned on page 110, because even main dealers can make 'mistakes', but once you've done that, and selected the main-dealer car you want, it's better to have an AA or RAC inspection carried out rather than carry out your own checks. But for many people, it's a question of saving money and buying privately, and that's what this Chapter is mainly about. But don't find yourself with the *worst* of both worlds...

Spot The Rogue Trader

One of the biggest dangers with buying privately is that you might encounter a real cheat: a trader masquerading as a private seller. Cars offered by such people are likely to be among the worst on offer, they may have had their mileometers tampered with and deep seated faults may have been cleverly concealed. Here's how to spot them:

• take note of the way traders often word their advertise-ments. Key phrases include: "a very clean car", "very straight", "a beautiful motorcar" and other glib phrases.

• when you telephone in response to an ad., *always* say, "I'm calling about the car..." If the person on the other end asks, "Which car?", put the 'phone down before the spiel starts.

• if you get past the telephone stage, take careful note of the attitude of the seller. Part-time, 'black economy' dealers often seem blase, even bored by the whole thing, and slicker than most private sellers.

• insist on looking at the Registration Document. If the seller isn't the registered keeper, why not?

How To Inspect A Used Vehicle

STAGE ONE: Even if you know very little about cars, you can root out the obvious no-hopers before arranging for a local main agent, AA or RAC inspection. The text in italics explains the problems.

• catch the light along all sides of the car. Can you see any ripples? Check for overspray inside wheel arches, inside engine bay and on tyres and trim. Does all the paint match? *All indicate poorly carried out crash repairs.*

• Look at the gaps between panels. Also, look very carefully inside the engine bay and inside the boot for evidence of rippling in the metal. Look low down, mainly in the vicinity of structural members. *Tell-tale signs of crash damage.*

STAGE TWO: If your car passes Stage One, look more closely at the bodywork - the most expensive part to repair.

• check the sills by lifting the carpets just inside the doors and also check the footwells, especially around the edges. *Rust!*

• look inside the engine bay especially at the tops of struts. *Check for corrosion.*

• check the bottoms of wings, the 'skirts' beneath front and rear bumpers and the tops of wing panels for corrosion. *Rust covered with filler will quickly burst through again.*

SPECIALIST SERVICE: It's hardly worth trying to check beneath a car without the use of a hoist. Leave it to the pro. inspection mentioned earlier, or see if you can persuade a local garage to lend or hire their hoist:

• check around spring mountings, the joints between floors and sills, all box-section 'chassis' members and anywhere that suspension components are fixed to the car's body structure.

• check all brake pipes and hoses. *Look for rubbing or corrosion.*

• look at the shock absorbers. *Fluid leakage means failure.*

• check the exhaust. *Look for rust, holes or patches.*

• examine each tyre carefully for bulges or splits. *Tyres worn more on one side than the other might mean that the car's tracking needs checking - easily adjustable - or it might indicate suspension damage, maybe from an accident.*

---

making it easy! If you are buying an older car which needs work doing to it, try making the owner an offer 'subject to MoT test'. Then, you can have the car tested as an inexpensive (though not necessarily complete) condition check.

Mechanical Components

• before starting up, remove the oil filler cap. *Grey sludge around the cap is a certain indicator that the engine is on its last legs.*

• pull out the dipstick. Is the oil level very low? Is the oil a dirty black and does it feel gritty between finger and thumb? *Not a well maintained car!* Does it have droplets of water on it? *Big problems! Probably a blown head gasket.*

• check inside the radiator cap (ONLY if the engine is cold!). Do you see anti-freeze colour? *Good!* Do you see rust? *Bad!* Do you see droplets of oil? *Disastrous! See previous paragraph.*

• start the car and note whether the starter motor sounds lively or whether it is struggling to keep up. *Could be duff battery; or tired starter motor.*

• undo and remove the oil filler cap again. (N.B. Most engines spray oil around in *copious* quantities. Ensure that you don't get covered!) *If oil mist chugs out, the engine bores are badly worn. Also...*

• ...look at the exhaust. Steam (especially in colder weather) and even water dripping out is no problem, although it should go away after the car has been driven. 'Rev' the engine, hard and several times. *If you see puffs or even clouds of black smoke (not grey steam), the engine is probably on the slippery slope.*

• does the oil pressure warning light flicker with engine cold? *Low oil pressure equals an engine rebuild?*

• bonnet open. Does the 'top' of the engine rattle on start up? *Mechanical tappets: adjustment needed.* If the rattle continues after 30 seconds, *the engine may need an expensive replacement camshaft.* Hydraulic tappets: *noise is always expensive!*

• rev the engine. Does it rattle in a deep, growly way, low down in the engine? *The big end and/or main bearings are gone - replacement engine time!*

Static Checks

• are the carpets wet? *water is leaking in. Windscreen seal leaks can often be cured easily. But if the car is old the screen surround may have corroded, requiring expensive welding. Alternatively, water coming in from beneath suggests that the car's lower structure has as much future as an old car park ticket. If water is leaking from the heater, remember that it can be expensive and tricky to replace.*

• seat rips can be a pain and devalue the car. *It can be difficult to find the right colour match on second hand seats.* Do your knees come up as your backside goes down? *The seat springing has gone.*

• can you live with headlining rips or severe discolouration? *It's difficult to clean easily and replacement is usually expensive.*

• take a *close* look at seat belts and mountings. *Life saver - and quite expensive to replace.*

• check that the heater works properly. *Or you'll end up hating the car!*

• take time to check every switch, accessory and electrical fitting on the car. *Replacements can be expensive.* Check that the stereo works - *and check that it's included with the car!*

• don't accept lame excuses when things don't work! *If things are so easy to fix, why haven't they been done already?*

• check the spare wheel and the condition (existence?) of the jack and toolkit. *More expense!*

• open and close windows and sunroof. *(Also look for stains around sunroof aperture - they can leak!)*

Finally, but perhaps most important of all, make sure that the person who is selling the car actually owns it!

• ask to see the Registration Document. *If it's not available it could be: the 'owner' has a) lost it; b) has it but it doesn't show the 'owner's' name because he is a trader; c) the car doesn't belong to the seller. If you can't see the Registration Document, walk away!*

• ask to see the owner's original purchase receipt and check that the car is owned by the 'owner' and is not subject to a finance agreement. See below. *IMPORTANT NOTE: You may be amazed to learn that, if you pay for a car that is subsequently found to belong to someone else, you will lose the car and the money!*

• check that the VIN (Vehicle Identification Number) shown on the Registration document is the same as those on the VIN plate riveted to the car. See "Fact File" later in this chapter for the precise location of these numbers. *If any of the numbers in these three locations are different, missing, or have obviously been tampered with, then under no circumstances consider buying the car unless the seller can provide an explanation, in writing, satisfactory to a third party, such as an AA or RAC inspector, or the Police!*

Spot The Rogue Car

Before buying *any* used car, check it out with HPI Autodata. (See Page 110.) A postal or telephone enquiry (cheques or credit card payments accepted) will (i) confirm that the vehicle details shown (make, model, colour, engine size, fuel type) are all correct, (ii) tell you if the vehicle is reported as stolen, or subject to an outstanding finance agreement, (iii) tell you if the vehicle has been logged as having a major insurance claim (not foolproof; many don't show up), (iv) identify vehicles which have had a registration plate change.

PART II: WHAT WEARS, AND WHEN

The following list provides a great way of checking what is *likely* to be worn on your vehicle, and at what stage it is likely to need replacement - useful when checking your own car, or when buying another. Please bear in mind that the mileages shown are only intended as an approximation of the lifespan of each component. In real life, some will wear out faster and some slower, of course but the chart below provides a useful rough guide.

> **SAFETY FIRST!**
> **Read and take note of Chapter1, Safety First! and the Safety information in Chapter 3 before carrying out any of these checks.**

COMPONENT:	COULD NEED REPLACEMENT AT:	CHECKS OR SYMPTOMS:
Alternator	70,000 miles	Fails without warning.
Battery	4 to 7 years (original); 1 to who-knows (non-original)	Goes flat, even though disconnected, or can't be charged with a battery charger.
Brake Pads - Front	15 to 20,000 miles	See Job 66.
Brake Pads/Shoes - Rear	35 to 40,000 miles	See Job 69.
Cambelt	36,000 miles	Should be renewed - see Job 113.
Clutch	Up to 75,000 normally	Check for slipping when pulling away, or hill climbing.
Diesel Glowplugs	60,000 miles	Engine reluctant to start from cold and smokes before warmed up.
Diesel Injectors	75,000 miles	Excessive smoke when engine warm; engine misfires.
Exhaust mountings	Rears can fracture after 2 or 3 years.	Examine visually; twist manually.
Exhaust pipe (Peugeot Parts) (non-original parts)	Up to 4 years 1 to 3 years	Examine visually - see Job 32; listen for blowing.
Shock absorbers Shock absorbers	(front) 40,000 miles (rear) 60,000 miles	Clean off and look for oil leaks. Grasp and twist, looking for wear in bushes top and bottom.
Starter motor	150,000 miles	Turns engine slowly or fails to engage when battery and connections in good condition.
Turbocharger	(diesel) 140,000 miles	Seal failure leads to engine oil being consumed - engine smokes through exhaust when turbo operates.
Tyres	(most models) 15 - 20,000 miles	Check visually, not forgetting the inner tyre walls and spare.

PART III - BUYING SPARES

One of the great advantages of DIY servicing is that you can choose which parts you buy, where you buy your parts, and how much you pay for them, whereas if the dealer services your car you buy their parts at their prices!

Of course, you must take care not to buy poor quality parts, but it's worth bearing in mind that many of the car makers' parts are the same as those available from 'independents'.

Buying The Right Parts

All manufacturers change the parts they use on the production line, often with startling frequency. The only way of ensuring that the parts you buy are the right ones for your car is to take your car's Vehicle Identification Number (VIN) and engine number with you when buying spares.

Main Dealers

Main dealers more than anyone else should be able to match your car's VIN number to the precise part you need, so have it to hand. This can also be the key to a more helpful approach by some Parts Department staff! Also, try to avoid calling on the parts department in the early mornings and other busy periods, and you may find that staff have more time to help you. Consumable items are almost certain to be too expensive from your main dealer. Try high street auto accessory stores or out-of-town Superstores for best prices.

Auto Accessory Stores

Local parts factors and big-name motor accessory shops can be extremely useful for obtaining servicing parts at short notice - many 'accessory' outlets open late in the evening, and on both days at weekends. You'll find that the high-street shops and Superstores will usually be open when you need them, their prices are usually the keenest of all, because they can buy-in in great quantities, and the quality of the parts is excellent from the best-known shops, since they use the same big-name manufacturers as many of the original car makers.

Buying Second-Hand

Purchasing any safety-related items second-hand - braking, steering or suspension parts - is something to avoid. That's not to decry buying second-hand altogether. Replacing a worn out distributor or carburettor, for instance, with a second-hand component that you know to be 'low mileage' can make a lot of sense. Equally, non-performance related items, such as wheel trims, interior trim and other interior parts can often be obtained at a fraction of the 'new' cost.

Reconditioned Parts

These are best obtained from reputable retail suppliers. When buying, always enquire about the terms of the guarantee. Don't buy if there isn't a good one! 'Exchange' alternators and starter motors are good value - but only buy from a reputable source.

Steering racks are invariably available as exchange items. Ensure that you rotate the operating shaft fully from lock to lock, feeling for any undue free play, roughness, stiffness, or 'notchiness' as you do so. Reject any units showing signs of any of these problems.

Tyres

We recommend buying only good quality radial ply tyres. Cheaper tyres rarely perform as well as top brands, even when they are the cheaper brand of a top manufacturer. Your car may steer more erratically, have less grip on cornering and braking and be noisier than if you pay the small extra amount required for top brand tyres - and they usually last longer, too. Remould tyres are available at lower initial cost, but life expectancy is not as long as with new tyres and we don't recommend them.

Shopping Around

If you want to buy good quality parts *and* save money, you must be prepared to shop around. Ring each of your chosen suppliers with a shopping list to hand, and your car's personal data, from the Auto-Biography at the front of this book, in front of you. Keep a written note of prices - including VAT, delivery etc - whether the parts are proper 'brand name' parts or not and - most importantly! - whether or not the parts you want are in stock. Parts expected 'soon' have been known never to materialise. A swivel pin in the hand is worth two in the bush. (Bad pun!)

FACT FILE: IDENTIFICATION NUMBERS

All manufacturers change the parts they use on the production line, often with startling frequency. The only way of ensuring that the parts you buy are the right ones for your car is to take your car's Vehicle Identification Number (VIN) and engine number with you when buying spares.

There are three main numbers you will need to know in order to buy parts and touch-up paint for your car. The VIN is your car's internationally unique number and tells your parts supplier exactly which model and year the car is. Quote the VIN whenever you buy spares for your car.

1A. The 205's VIN plate is positioned on top of the left-hand wing (as you look to the rear of the car) just in front of the bulkhead in the engine bay, and the number should be the same as that shown on your

vehicle documents. Look for the second number (the third box) down on the plate.

1B. The VIN number is also stamped onto the bodyshell at manufacture and is found on the bulkhead panel just in front of

the air intake grille, and just behind the VIN plate as shown.

2. The engine number will be found on the front of the engine block, at the joint with the gearbox (on all but XU-type engines), embossed onto one of two aluminium plates; the engine number is on the non-printed plate. On XU engines the plate is found on the left-hand end of the engine, next to the cam-belt cover. A few engines may have the prefix G1, 2 or 3 - these are identified to the XU, XV and XY engines and can be regarded as such.

3. If you need an exact paint colour match, you'll need the car's paint code number (arrow 4). Although the VIN plate will carry the basic colour code, the paint/trim code plate will contain precise details of the shade and the type of trim fitted. It is situated on

the front 'slam' panel, to the right of the bonnet catch, and is usually painted in the body colour. Most aerosol paints won't relate to this number, although at least one brand claims to be able to produce cans matched to your car's code colour, to special order. Alternatively, have your local paint factor mix a small quantity of matching paint for you. (Illustration, courtesy Peugeot Talbot Motor Co Plc)

Please read the whole of the Introduction to this Chapter before carrying out any work on your car.

SERVICING YOUR CAR

CHAPTER 3 - SERVICING YOUR CAR

Everyone wants to own a car that starts first time, runs reliably and lasts longer than the average. And there's no magic about how to put your car into that category, it's all a question of thorough maintenance! If you follow the Service Jobs listed here or even if you have a garage or mechanic do it for you - you can almost *guarantee* that your car will still be going strong when others have fallen by the wayside... or the hard shoulder.

If you want your car to be as well looked after as possible, you'll follow the Jobs shown here, but if you don't want to go all the way, you can pick and choose from the most essential items in the list. But do bear in mind that the Jobs we recommend are there for some very good reasons:

◆ **body maintenance** is rarely included in most service schedules. We believe it to be essential.

◆ **preventative maintenance** figures very high on our list of priorities. And that's why so many of our service jobs have the word "Check..." near the start!

We think it's very important to keep things as straight-forward as possible. And where you see this heading, you'll know there's an extra tip to help 'make it easy' for you!

The 'Catch-up' Service

When you first buy a used car, you never know for sure just how well it's been looked after. Even one with a full service history is unlikely to have been serviced as thoroughly as one with a Porter Manual Service History! So, if you want to catch-up on all the servicing that may have been neglected on your car, just work through the entire list of Service Jobs listed for the longest term servicing jobs listed in this Manual, and your car will be bang up to date and serviced as well as you could hope for. Do allow several days for all of this work, not least because it will almost certainly throw up a number of extra jobs - potential faults that have been lurking beneath the surface - all of which will need putting right before you can 'sign off' your car as being in tip-top condition.

The Service History

Those people fortunate enough to own a new car, or one that has been well maintained from new will have the opportunity to keep a 'Service History' of their car, usually filled in by a main dealer. Now you can keep your own complete record, using the tick list in the Appendix at the back of this book.

Your car's Service History will then be more complete and detailed than any manufacturer's service record, with the extra bonus that there is space for you to keep a record of all those extras: New tyres; replacement exhaust; extra accessories, so if your battery goes down only 11 months after buying it, you'll be able to look up where and when you bought it.

RAISING THE CAR

Raising The Car Before Working On It

RAISING A CAR - SAFELY!
You will often need to raise your car off the ground in order to carry out the Service Jobs shown here. To start off with, here's what you must never do - never work beneath a car held on a jack, not even a trolley jack. Quite a number of deaths have been caused by a car slipping off a jack while someone has been working beneath. On the other hand, the safest way is by raising a car on a proprietary brand of ramps. Sometimes, there is no alternative but to use axle stands. Please read all of the following information and act upon it!

When using car ramps:

(I) Make absolutely certain that the ramps are parallel to the wheels of the car and that the wheels are exactly central on each ramp.

Always have an assistant watch both sides of the car as you drive up. Drive up to the end 'stops' on the ramps but never over them!

Apply the hand brake firmly, put the car in first or reverse gear, or 'Park', in the case of an automatic.

(II) Chock both wheels remaining on the ground, both in front and behind so that the car can't move in either direction.

INSIDE INFORMATION: wrap a strip of carpet into a loop around the first 'rung' of the ramps and drive over the doubled-up piece of carpet on the approach to the ramps. This prevents the ramps from skidding away, as they are inclined to do, as the car is driven on to them.

I

When using axle stands:

On·other occasions, you might need to work on the car while it is supported on an axle stand or a pair of axle stands. These are somewhat less stable than ramps so take greater care when working beneath them. In particular:

• ensure that the axle stand is on flat, stable ground, never on a surface where one side can sink in to the ground.

• ensure that the car is on level ground and that the hand brake is on and the transmission in 'P' or PARK after chocking those wheels remaining on the ground.

II

When using a trolley jack:

We recommend that you invest in a small trolley jack if you don't already own one; the car's wheel changing jack is often too unstable and not suitable for anything other than wheel changing.

(III) Ensure that the ground is sufficiently clear and smooth for the trolley jack wheels to roll as the car is raised and lowered, otherwise it could slip off the jack. Use the reinforced jacking points adjacent to the sills - see XI below for their location.

III

(IV) Position front axle stands beneath the subframe - placing them towards the rear of the subframe will provide plenty of space when working beneath the engine and gearbox.

(V) At the rear of the car, position an axle stand at each end of the suspension cross-beam, taking care not to allow the head of the stand to damage any cables or brackets fixed to it.

Be especially careful when applying force to a spanner or when pulling hard on anything, when the car is supported off the ground. It is all too easy to move the car so far that it topples off the axle stands. And remember that if a car falls on you, YOU COULD BE KILLED!

Whenever working beneath a car, have someone primed to keep an eye on you! If someone pops out to see how you are getting on every quarter of an hour or so, it could be enough to save your life!

Do remember that, in general, a car will be more stable when only one wheel is removed and one axle stand used than if two wheels are removed in conjunction with two axle stands. You are strongly advised never to work on the car with all four wheels off the ground, on four axle stands. The car would then be very unstable and dangerous to work beneath.

Raising the Car in an Emergency

It happens too often - a roadside puncture, probably in the dark, probably in the rain, the spare is flat, you don't know where the car jack is, or the wheelbrace, and even if you did you don't know where the jack should go, and the wheel bolts are far too tight to be shifted by that bit of bent rod they call a wheelbrace! If you've never done it before, changing a wheel can be a daunting prospect but in practice isn't difficult; practice the wheel-change routine at home first, in the safety and comfort of your driveway, before the worst happens to you.

SAFETY FIRST!
Wheel changing jacks can be dreadfully unstable! Take great care not to get any part of your body under the car when supported by one of these jacks.

(VI) START by finding where the jack and the wheelbrace are normally stowed - on all 205s they are tucked inside the left-hand inner wing, behind the headlight - make sure the securing wing-nut doesn't become seized: oil it occasionally.

(VII) The spare wheel is held in a cradle beneath the luggage area and is secured by a bolt protruding through the floor - the wheel brace fits this bolt which, when turned, lowers the carrier and wheel to the ground. (Illustration, courtesy Peugeot Talbot Motor Co Plc)

CHECK that the spare hasn't gone flat, checking it every week, along with the other wheels/tyres.

PREPARE by ensuring that in the boot and/or glovebox you have an old waterproof, something to kneel on, rag to clean your hands if necessary, but also protective gloves, and a torch.

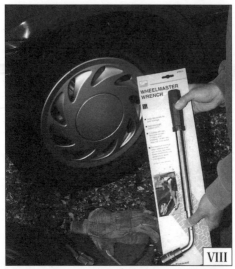

(VIII) Wheel bolts should be done up to a specified degree of tightness, but all too often they're done up by a chap behaving like a gorilla with a toothache! Give yourself a better chance by buying one of these extendible wrenches, complete with the right-sized socket to fit your wheel bolts. Its superior strength and leverage will shift wheel bolts that the car-kit brace wouldn't even look at - it's an absolute 'must', not just for those who haven't got the strength of a raging gorilla but to replace that feeble wheel brace in the boot, for everyone!

(IX) In many instances, you will first have to lever off a wheeltrim - or plastic caps over the bolts that look like the real thing but are not! The car wheelbrace has a hooked end made for the job -simply use it to pull the cover away, as shown.

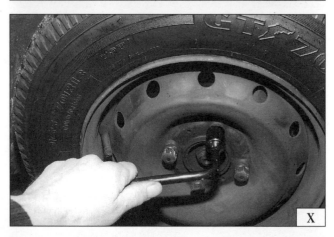

(X) With the wheel still on the ground, loosen the wheel bolts. For your physical well-being you should always bear down on the wheelbrace, rather than pull it upwards. If you try slackening the bolts after you've raised the wheel, all you'll do is rotate the wheel, not the bolt!

(XI) Make sure now that you know exactly where and how the jack locates beneath the car. The jacking-points on 205s (arrowed) are identical on both sides of the car. At each point there is a notch cut in the sill-edge which locates in the head of the jack.

XII

(XII) Unfold and wind the handle clockwise to extend the jack, making sure it is kept as vertical as possible, although its angle may change slightly as the jack is extended.

Remember to carry a piece of timber in the boot to be placed beneath the jack to spread the load and prevent it from sinking into soft ground. Once the car is raised, have the handbrake on. There are purpose-made chocks you can wedge each side of the wheel opposite to the one you are changing, to guard against the car rolling. In an emergency, use any old pieces of wood or bricks that you can find. Wind the jack handle until the required wheel is clear of the ground, remembering that if the tyre is flat, you need enough clearance for a wheel with a fully pumped up tyre - do not put any part of your body beneath a car which is supported only on a jack.

XIII

(XIII) SAFETY FIRST! and INSIDE INFORMATION Always place the spare wheel, or the wheel you've just removed, under the car: partly for safety to help guard against being crushed and partly so that if the car topples off the wheel-change jack (and they DO, especially on soft ground) you'll be able to reposition the jack and start again.

Once the required wheel is clear of the ground, fully undo the bolts, leaving one 'at the top' until last so you can get your balance and a secure grip before lifting away the wheel. It can be a bit of a struggle to try to locate the wheel on something (maybe some sort of projection on the hub/drum face) while you attempt to align the bolt holes and insert at least one bolt with one hand while steadying the wheel with the other!

Nip the bolts up finger-tight, then lower the wheel to the ground for final tightening, working diagonally, a little at a time, on each bolt; do them up as tight as you can, using all your strength if it's the car-kit wheelbrace, slightly less than full strength if it's the extended wrench.

(XIV) The correct way of tightening wheel bolts is to use a torque wrench - strongly recommended if your car is fitted with alloy wheels. Check the correct figure with your dealer, if you don't know.

XIV

making it easy!

i) Because its difficult to locate wheels held on with bolts, have your local garage supply you with two pieces of threaded rod - wheel retaining bolts with heads cut off would be ideal. You can screw them into two of the holes in the hub, 'hang' the wheel on them while you put in the 'proper' wheel bolts to the other holes, then unscrew them with your fingers and fit the two remaining wheel retaining bolts. Remember to carry them with you! ii) You can also try levering the wheel up into place with a shovel, a length of wood or anything else you can lay your hands on, by the roadside.

FACT FILE: ENGINE BAY LAYOUTS

Engine Identification:

Throughout this book, engines are referred to by their type, i.e. 'XV', 'TU' etc. This refers to the prefix assigned to the various engine types by Peugeot and can be determined by checking the engine identification plate - see *Chapter 2, Identification Numbers* for its location. If the identification plate is missing or unreadable, it is possible to determine your engine type by comparing with those shown below, or by consulting your owner's handbook. If all else fails, consult your Peugeot dealer, who will be pleased to confirm the engine type for you.

There are five main engine bay layouts in the 205 range, as follows:

2. XU ENGINES

4. DIESEL ENGINES

1. TU ENGINES

3. XV, XW & XY ENGINES

5. TURBO DIESEL

Key:
1. Engine oil dipstick.
2. Engine oil filler cap.
3. Engine oil filter cartridge.
4. Brake fluid reservoir/ master cylinder.
5. Battery.
6. Screen wash reservoir.
7. Power steering fluid reservoir (if applicable).
8. Air cleaner housing.
9. Fuel filter (petrol fuel injection engines only).
10. Manual stop lever on injector pump (diesel engines only).
11. Drivebelts.
12. Vacuum pump.

(Illustrations, courtesy Peugeot Talbot Motor Co plc.)

Every 500 Miles, Weekly or Before Long Journeys

These are the regular checks that you need to carry out to keep your car safe and reliable. They don't include the major Service Jobs but they should be carried out as part of every 'proper' service.

Every 500 Miles - The Engine Bay

1A

□ **Job 1. Engine oil level.**

Check the engine's oil level with the car on level ground.

1A. On XV, XW and XY engines, the dipstick is positioned towards the front of the engine behind the air filter housing; on XU engines it is behind and to the top of the engine as you face the front of the car; on TU and diesel engines (as shown) it is at the front left-hand side - see Engine Bay Layouts on page 20 if in doubt. Lift out the dipstick, wipe it with a clean cloth, push it back in and lift out again. Take a look at the level of the oil on the dipstick. You might have to do this three or four times before you can see a clear reading - the oil on the stick sometimes 'smears' as the stick is pulled out.

1B

1B. The oil level must be maintained above the 'MIN' mark or lower notch on the dipstick. Approximately one pint, or just over half a litre, will raise the level from the 'MIN' to the 'MAX' mark.

On XV, XW & XY engines the oil cap is located at the top of a 'filler tube' fitted to the valve cover at the rear of the engine the cap is a simple push-fit.

1C. On XU petrol and XUD diesel engines the cap is located towards the centre of the engine bay - the dipstick passes through it - and is released by the two spring clips

1C

1D. On TU series engines the cap is located on the valve cover and is a 'twist-off' bayonet type.

1E. Add oil slowly to avoid spills; a funnel-measure like that shown is useful for topping-up as it allows a check to be made on oil consumption.

On all models, check the ground over which the car has been parked for evidence of oil or other fluid leaks. If any leaks are found, do not drive the car without first establishing where the leaks have come from - they could have come from a major failure in the braking system which will probably call for **SPECIALIST SERVICE** attention.

1D

1E

☐ **Job 2. Check coolant level.**

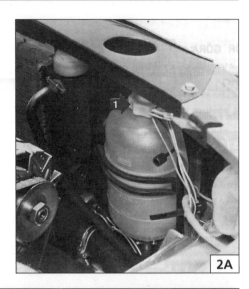
2A

SAFETY FIRST!
i) The coolant level should only be checked WHEN THE SYSTEM IS COLD . If you remove the pressure cap when the engine is hot, the release of pressure can cause the water in the system to boil and spurt several feet into the air with the risk of severe scalding. ii) Take precautions to prevent antifreeze coming into contact with the skin or eyes. If this should happen, rinse immediately with plenty of water.

2A. On XV, XW and XY engined models the coolant system expansion bottle is positioned below the front 'slam'-panel, towards the left as you stand in front of the car. The translucent bottle is provided with 'MIN' and 'MAX' marks so the level can be checked without removing the cap.

2B. On GTI, diesel and TU type engines the expansion tank (bottle-shaped on earlier models) is located on the bulkhead at the rear and to the right of the engine bay. The tank or bottle is translucent and marked with MIN and MAX positions.

2B

ALL TYPES: If necessary, top up the system with a mixture of 50% antifreeze and water to the 'MAX' level mark on the expansion bottle.

☐ **Job 3. Brake fluid level.**

3A. The transparent brake fluid reservoir is on the top of the master cylinder located in the rear left-hand corner of the engine bay. 'MIN' and 'MAX' level marks are provided to check the level without disturbing the cap and risking the ingress of dirt or grit.

3A

SAFETY FIRST!
i) If brake fluid should come into contact with the skin or eyes, rinse immediately with plenty of water. ii) It is acceptable for the brake fluid level to fall slightly during normal use, but if it falls significantly below the 'MIN' mark on the reservoir it indicates a leak or an internal seal failure. Stop using the car and seek specialist advice immediately. iii) If you let dirt get into the hydraulic system it can cause brake failure. Wipe the filler cap clean before removing. iv) You should only ever use new brake fluid from an air-tight container. Old fluid absorbs moisture and this could cause the brakes to fail when carrying out an emergency stop or other heavy use of the brakes - just when you need them most and are least able to do anything about it, in fact.

3B

3B. If topping-up is necessary, wipe the top clean before removing the cap. Take care not to damage the wiring to the low-level warning switch and allow the level-indicator tube time to drain.

3C. Top up to the 'MAX' mark on the side of the reservoir, using fresh fluid from a sealed container - brake fluid absorbs water, which reduces its efficiency and can cause corrosion, so always use new fluid.

making it easy! 3D. Should the push-on connectors become disturbed, they can be replaced on the two terminals either way round. Also, before lifting the cap clear of the reservoir, allow the fluid in the tube on the underside of the cap to drain back into the reservoir rather than around your engine bay.

Check the brake fluid level warning light. With the handbrake off chock the wheels first and place the gearbox in first gear (or 'P' in the case of an automatic) - and the ignition switched on, lift the reservoir cap and its float clear of the fluid. The warning light on the dash should light up. If it does not, and the fluid level is satisfactory, have the circuit checked by a specialist without delay.

INSIDE INFORMATION: i) Check the ground on which the car has been parked, especially beneath the engine bay and each road wheel, for evidence of oil, clutch or brake fluid leaks. If any are found, investigate further before driving the car. ii) Brake fluid will damage painted surfaces if allowed to come into contact. Take care not to spill any but, if there is an accident, refit the master cylinder reservoir cap and wash off any accidental spillage immediately with hot soapy water.

☐ **Job 4. Check windscreen wash level.**

4A. The washer reservoir on all models is located on the right-hand side of the engine bay beside the battery; the cap is a simple push-on fit. Top-up with a mixture of water and screenwash additive that will clean the screen in summer and prevent freezing in winter.

4B. Check the level, and top-up if required, the rear washer fluid reservoir - it is located on the right-hand side of the luggage compartment.

Every 500 Miles - Around the Car

☐ **Job 5. Check tyre pressures.**

5. Use a reliable pressure gauge to check the pressure in each tyre, including the spare. Always check pressures with the tyres cold, never just after using the car which warms up the tyres and increases their pressures.

500 MILEWEEKLY SERVICE

☐ Job 6. Check front lights and indicators.

Check the operation of the sidelights, indicators and headlights, on both full and dipped beam. If one sidelight, or one headlight beam fails to work on either side, the bulb has probably failed.

6A

HEADLIGHTS

6A. After removing the rubber or plastic cover (2), pull-away the three-way terminal connector (1) from the bulb contacts; free the spring clip (3) which holds the bulb (4) in position.

6B. Hold the bulb by the contacts and lift it out to examine the filaments. *INSIDE INFORMATION: if the bulb feels loose on reassembly, gently bend the clip slightly to give it more grip.*

6B

SIDELIGHTS

6C. The sidelight bulb-holder is a simple push-fit in the headlight reflector, while the bulb is also a push-fit in the holder.

 If you touch a halogen headlight or driving light with bare fingers, the microscopic transfer of grease will shorten its life. Handle with a piece of tissue paper if the original wrapping is no longer there. If the bulb is touched - no worries! Just wipe carefully clean with methylated spirit on a fresh, clean tissue or cloth.

6C

INDICATORS

6D. The direction indicator bulb-holder is a bayonet-type fitting in its reflector - turn the holder anti-clockwise to detach it. The bulb is also a bayonet fitting in the holder, again turn anti-clockwise to remove it.

6D

DRIVING LIGHTS

GTI MODELS ONLY

6E. Remove the two screws from the lens surround and pull the reflector assembly forward to give access to the bulb-holder and connector; disconnect the wires. The bulb is retained by a spring clip identical to that on the headlights - squeeze the 'ears' together and swing it clear to release the bulb. NOTE: Hold the bulb by the metal base, not the glass envelope. (Illustration, courtesy Peugeot Talbot Motor Co Plc)

6E

☐ Job 7. Check side indicator repeaters.

There are two types of side repeater; the early type is removed by reaching up behind the wing and squeezing the two plastic lugs on the rear of the holder, when it can be pushed forwards and out. Separate the bulb-holder from the lens by twisting anti-clockwise.

7. On later types the lens is simply turned a quarter-turn to the left and pulled through the aperture in the wing.

On both types the bulb is a simple push-fit in the holder.

7

Job 8. Check rear lights.

8A. The rear light cluster contains the following bulbs; (1) Indicator (21 watt); (2) Tail light/stop light (5/21 watt); (3) Reverse light (21 watt); (4) Reflector. The rear fog light (5) is positioned within the rear bumper, as is the rear fog light on models from 1989. (Illustration, courtesy Peugeot Talbot Motor Co Plc)

8B. Access to the bulbs is gained by undoing the two screws at the top of the lens panel then tilting and lifting it away from the bottom tabs. Remove the bulbs by pushing-in and turning anti-clockwise.

REAR FOG LIGHTS

8C. The rear fog light lens-cover is secured by two screws, one at each end. With the screws undone the bulb can be removed by pushing-in slightly and turning anti-clockwise.

REVERSING LIGHT

MODELS FROM 1989 ONLY

On these later models the reversing light is separate from the main cluster and is located in the rear valence. Bulb changing is the same as for the rear fog light described above.

Job 9. Number plate lights.

9. These lights are located beneath the rear bumper. To remove the bulbs, twist-off the plastic lens, then push-in and turn the bulb anti-clockwise.

Job 10. Interior lights.

10A. Carefully prise-out the interior light from the fitting in the roof using a small flat-bladed screwdriver. The appearance and type varies between models.

10B. The bulb is the 'festoon' type and is held between two sprung contacts - hold the bulb and push slightly towards one contact and lift out.

FACT FILE: FUSES

INSIDE INFORMATION: If a complete 'set' of bulbs fails to operate (and especially if other electrical components fail at the same time) check the fuses before suspecting any other fault. If a replacement fuse blows, you probably have a circuit fault. Seek specialist advice immediately. If the fuse protecting the circuit has not blown, it may be that a relay has failed. In this case, seek SPECIALIST SERVICE.

SAFETY FIRST!

Make sure that all the electrical circuits are switched off before removing or replacing a fuse. NEVER try to 'cure' a fault by fitting a fuse with a higher amperage rating than the one specified.

The fuses are colour coded, red for 10 amp, blue for 15 amp, yellow for 20 amp, neutral or clear for 25 amp and green for 30 amp. A blown fuse is clearly identified by a break in the wire.

A. On all cars, the main fuse box is located under the fascia on the left-hand side of the vehicle. Release the catch (1) and tilt the assembly down for access.

A

Make sure you identify the correct fuse for the circuit which has failed. Some circuits, such as the radio, may have a separate, additional line-fuse in the wiring to them. Refer to your dealer or the owner's handbook to check.

The following list details the fuses and the circuits/accessories protected by them - note that not all of these may apply to your car as some are optional extras or special equipment.

FUSE Nos., Rating (in AMPS) and CIRCUITS:

1. 10 AMP - Reverse lamp; tachometer; dashlight dimmer; fuel gauge; 'water-in-fuel' sensor (diesel only); dash warning lights.
2. 25 AMP - Direction indicators; fuel gauge; seat heaters; additional heater/ventilation pump; dash gauges; heater/ventilation; air conditioning; warning lights.
3. 25 AMP - Reading light; brake/stop lights; windscreen wash/wipe (front & rear); tachometer; headlight washer; car radio & accessories; glove box light; rear screen heater relay.
4. 15 AMP - Driving/spot lights.
5. 10 AMP - Hazard warning lights.
6. NOT USED
7. 25 AMP - Clock; interior lighting; boot light; central locking; car radio (permanent 'live' connection); power supply to towbar.
8. 30 AMP - Horn; rear screen demister/heater; cigar lighter.
9. 20 AMP - Front electric windows.
10. 5 AMP - Rear fog light.
11. 5 AMP - Rear side lights.
12. NOT USED
13. 5 AMP - Fascia panel lights; front side lights.
14. 5 AMP - Fuel pump.

B

B. Certain later models also have four additional fuses located under the bonnet, adjacent to the battery; these are:
A. 30 AMP - ABS braking system (when fitted).
B. 15 AMP - ABS control unit (when fitted).
C. 30 AMP - Engine fan.
D. 10 AMP - Lambda probe (catalyst models only).
(Illustrations, courtesy Peugeot Talbot Motor Co Plc)

☐ **Job 11. Check windscreen wipers.**

11A. The blade is removed from the arm by squeezing together the 'U' shaped plastic connector-block and sliding the blade from the hooked end of the arm.

11A

11B

11B. The arm is removed from the pivot by pulling-back the plastic cover and undoing the retaining nut...

11C. ... when the arm can then be lifted away. Ensure that the blade is in the correct position on the windscreen and that the arm is fitted firmly to the splines on the pivot-shaft, when replacing.

11C

☐ **Job 12. Windscreen washers.**

12A. If the screen washer jets are not properly aimed, they can be adjusted with a pin inserted in the jet hole as shown. If one of the jets is blocked, it can usually be freed with a piece of thin wire (untwist some from the end of a length of multi-strand electric cable).

12B. Also check the jet on the rear tailgate, as shown in 12A and also the headlight washer jets, if fitted.

INSIDE INFORMATION: If the washer motor works, but the washers don't, suspect a break in the plastic supply tube: It becomes brittle with age and is particularly prone to breaking at the top of the tailgate on Hatchbacks - look inside the black convoluted covering.

Every 1,500 Miles - or Every Month, whichever comes first

Every 1,500 Miles - The Engine Bay

☐ **Job 13. Check battery electrolyte level.**

SAFETY FIRST!
i) The gas given off by a battery is highly explosive. Never smoke, use a naked flame or allow a spark to occur in the battery compartment. Never disconnect the battery (it can cause sparking) with the battery caps removed. ii) Batteries contain sulphuric acid. If the acid comes into contact with the skin or eyes, wash immediately with copious amounts of cold water and seek medical advice. iii) Do not check the battery levels within half an hour of the battery being charged with a separate battery charger because the addition of fresh water could then cause the highly acid and corrosive electrolyte to flood out of the battery.

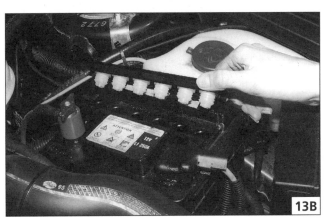

13A. The battery is located in the engine bay, on the right-hand side as you look towards the rear of the car.

13B. Remove the battery caps or covers and check the level of the electrolyte, i.e. the fluid inside each battery cell. The plates inside the battery should just be covered with electrolyte. Note that this only applies to batteries with removable caps, not to the 'Maintenance Free' batteries fitted to many 205s when new.

making it easy! You may find it useful to use a small electric torch to throw some light into the battery compartments. If you have difficulty seeing the electrolyte surface, tap the battery to make the liquid shimmer.

13C. If the level has fallen, top up with distilled water. NEVER use tap water, as it can destroy your battery. After replacing the covers, dry off the top of the battery. Check security of battery clamp at the base of the battery. If the terminals are furry with crystals or corroded, clean them by pouring boiling water over them. Dry the battery top and coat the terminals with Vaseline (petroleum jelly).

INSIDE INFORMATION: i) Once water is mixed with acid inside the battery it won't freeze. So, in extremely cold weather, run the car (out of doors) so that you put a charge into the battery and this will mix the fresh water with the electrolyte, cutting out the risk of freezing and a cracked battery case. ii) If your battery persistently goes flat it may indicate a fault in the charging circuit, but it may be that the battery is nearing the end of its useful life. You can check the battery by measuring the specific gravity of the electrolyte - see Job 84.

Job 14. Check horn.

Operate the horn push to check that the horn sounds. If it does not, and the fuse has not blown, check the connections to the horn itself, which is mounted beneath the left-hand headlight. If the connections are poor, remake them, but remember that, with some circuits, one of the wires to the horn is live whenever the ignition is on. To be completely safe, disconnect battery before removing either cable from the horn, or seek Specialist Service.

FACT FILE: DISCONNECTING THE BATTERY

Many vehicles depend on a constant power supply from the battery and you can find yourself in all sorts of trouble if you simply disconnect the battery on those vehicles. You might find that the car alarm will go off, you could find that the engine management system forgets all it ever 'learned' and the car will feel very strange to drive until it has re-programmed itself, and you could find that your radio refuses to operate again unless you key in the correct code. And if you've bought the car second-hand and don't know the code, you would have to send the set back to the manufacturer for re-programming. So, on later cars with engine management systems you must ensure that the vehicle has a constant power supply even though the battery is removed. To do so, you will need a separate 12 volt battery supply. You could put a self tapping screw into the positive lead near the battery terminal before disconnecting it, and put a positive connection to your other battery via this screw. But you would have to be EXTREMELY CAREFUL to wrap insulation tape around the connection so that no short is caused. The negative terminal on the other battery would also have to be connected to the cars bodywork.

A better way is to use something like the Sykes-Pickavant Computer Saver shown here. Clip the cables to your spare battery and plug into your cigarette lighter. (You may have to turn the ignition switch to the 'Auxiliary' setting to allow the

cigarette lighter to function).

You have to hold in the red button on the Computer Saver while inserting it into the cigarette lighter, and if two green lights still show after the button is released, you have a good connection and your battery can now be disconnected and removed.

Be sure not to turn on any of the car's equipment while the auxiliary battery is connected.

Every 1,500 Miles - Around the Car

Job 15. Check tyre treads.

15. Check the tyres for tread depth, using a depth gauge and note that, in the UK, the minimum legal tread depth is 1.6 mm. Tyres are not at their safest at that level and you may want to replace them earlier. Also check both sides of each tyre for uneven wear, bulges or other damage to the side walls. Raise each wheel of the ground, using an axle stand, otherwise you won't be able to see the inside of each tyre properly, nor will you be able to check that part of the tyre which is in contact with the ground.

16

SAFETY FIRST!
Tyres which show uneven wear tell their own story, if only you know how to speak the language! If any tyre is worn more on one side than another, consult your main dealer or a tyre specialist. It probably means that your suspension or steering is out of adjustment - probably a simple tracking job but conceivably symptomatic of suspension damage, so have it checked. If a tyre is worn more in the centre or on the edges, it could mean that your tyre pressures are wrong but, once again, have the car checked. Incorrectly inflated tyres wear rapidly, can cause the car's handling to become dangerous and can even cause the car to consume noticeably more fuel. When checking your tyres, don't forget to include the spare.

☐ Job 16. Check spare wheel.

16. The spare wheel lives under the floor of the luggage compartment. Check the tyre pressure with a reliable gauge. We suggest that you keep the pressure a few psi above that of your road tyres and reduce to the proper level if necessary, should you have to use it. When allocating the wheel as a spare you should have checked that the tread depth was legal, as shown in *Job 15.*

17

making it easy! You should inflate the spare tyre to the maximum pressure recommended for high speed or load running. Then, if you have a puncture while on a journey, you'll be okay. It's always easier to carry a tyre pressure gauge with you and let some air out than put some in.

☐ Job 17. Touch-up paintwork.

17. Touch-up stone chips with a small brush to prevent rust. If rust is already showing, treat first with a proprietary rust killer, following the instructions on the package. Allow new paint to harden before polishing.

18

☐ Job 18. Valet interior.

18. Use a vacuum cleaner with a flexible hose to clean the upholstery and carpets. If you haven't got a suitable vacuum cleaner, use one at a garage valeting station. They are much more powerful than the small type which plugs into the car's cigar lighter socket.

☐ Job 19. Improve visibility.

19. After leathering off the windows, go over them with a proprietary glass cleaner to make them sparkling clean. You will be surprised at the difference this makes. Also, clean the door and interior mirrors and check them for any damage.

19

Every 3,000 Miles - or Every Three Months, whichever comes first

Every 3,000 Miles - The Engine Bay

First carry out Jobs 1 to 5

☐ **Job 20. Check alternator drive belt.**

PETROL ENGINED MODELS WITHOUT POWER STEERING, UP TO 1990

XV, XW, XY ENGINES

20A. The belt is located on the left of the engine (as you look into the engine bay); the alternator is mounted so that adjustment can be made from above, by slackening the nut and bolt shown and tensioning the belt by moving the alternator upwards, tightening the bolt when tension is correct.

TU AND XU PETROL AND XUD DIESEL ENGINES UP TO 1989

20B. The belt is positioned low on the left-side of the engine and access to the belt adjuster is gained by removing this plastic panel (arrowed) from the inner wing, via four screws.

20C. Check the tension of the belt by deflecting it with firm finger or thumb pressure at a point halfway along the bottom 'run' of the belt. The amount of movement should be no more than 12mm (0.5in.). This example is the 'toothed-belt' type.

20D. Also check the general condition of the belt, looking for signs of cracking and frayed edges, and also for signs of 'polishing' of the belt's surface that can lead to 'squeal'. That shown is a later type of 'ribbed' belt.

ADJUSTMENT - TU & XU PETROL ENGINES

20E. Slacken the clamp nut (arrowed) and with a spanner turn the tensioning bolt at the end of the bracket, as shown; clockwise tightens, anti-clockwise slackens the belt.

20F

ADJUSTMENT - DIESEL ENGINES

20F. Adjustment is made from inside the engine bay; first slacken the adjuster clamp-nut and bolt (arrowed) - a half turn or so is usually enough.

20G. Using a spanner on the adjuster bolt, tension the belt by turning clockwise. Tighten the clamp nut and bolt when the correct tension is achieved.

20G

20H. On some models, where air conditioning and/or power steering is fitted: Slacken the bolts (2 and 3) and adjust the belt via the adjuster bolt (1). (Illustration, courtesy Peugeot Talbot Motor Co Plc)

> For owners of all diesel engined cars, Porter Manuals top selling **DIESEL CAR ENGINES SERVICE GUIDE** is the complete guide to how diesel engines work, buying a diesel, servicing all types in detail, and much more besides.

☐ **Job 21. Check vacuum pump drive belt.**

making it easy!

> Use a length of wood (such as the handle of a hammer) to apply sideways pressure to the alternator body (as near to the drive end bracket as possible) moving it away from the engine against belt tension. Provided the alternator bracket bolt hasn't been loosened too much, the alternator should 'stay-put' while the adjuster-stay nut and bolt are tightened. However, if you find this procedure difficult (it takes practice!) ask an assistant to hold the wooden lever while you tighten the bolt. Don't overtighten!

DIESEL ENGINED MODELS ONLY

21A. Check the tension of the brake vacuum pump as shown - the belt should deflect no more than 5mm at the mid-point in its run.

21B. If adjustment is required; first slacken the clamp-bolt as shown, then push the pump rearwards to tension the belt, tightening the clamp-bolt when the correct tension is achieved.

20H

21A

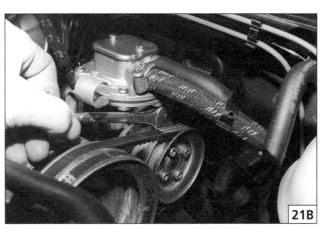

21B

☐ **Job 22. Drain fuel filter.**

DIESEL ENGINES ONLY

> *SAFETY FIRST!*
> *Whenever you are dealing with diesel fuel, it's essential to protect your hands by wearing plastic gloves.*

Drain the diesel fuel filter to remove any water residue.

22A

INSIDE INFORMATION: The fuel filter on diesel engines is designed so that any water which passes through it will collect at the bottom of the filter housing, immediately above the drain plug. This means that any water present will be drained first and the drain plug can be closed as soon as fuel begins to flow. Under normal conditions, the amount of water likely to be present is usually very small, although under extreme conditions of high humidity or widely varying day-to-night temperatures, more will be present, so the careful diesel owner may wish to check the filter every 3,000 miles.

CARS UP TO 1989

22A. The fuel filter is located at the rear/left corner of the engine bay. Start by connecting a short length of hose to the drain tap at the bottom of the filter - place a container beneath it to catch any fuel and/or water that will drain off.

22B. Loosen the bleed screw at the top of the filter housing ('A') then turn the bottom drain plug to allow the contents of the filter to drain. Tighten the bleed and drain screws afterwards. If more than a few millilitres of fuel are drained, it will be necessary to bleed any air from the filter by operating the plunger ('B') with the bleed screw ('A') opened, until resistance is felt and fuel dribbles from the bleed screw, indicating that the filter is full.

22B

CARS FROM 1990

22C. A different design of filter housing is used on these models; the bleed screw is at 'A', while a plastic drain tube is provided, 'B'. To drain the filter, simply turn the bleed screw until clean fuel issues from the drain tube. DON'T drain fuel away to the ground. Catch it in a suitable container and dispose of it at your local authority waste disposal centre.

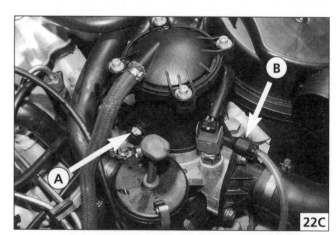

22C

☐ **Job 23. Renew diesel engine oil.**

DIESEL ENGINES ONLY

OPTIONAL: This job is specified by Peugeot at 5,000 miles but with no time limit; we include it here regardless, but if your car only covers a small mileage, say 1,000 miles or less in three months, then you may want to include it in the *Every 6,000 Miles or Every Six Months* checks described later in this chapter.

Refer to *Job 45* later in this chapter for precise instructions - the diesel engine is identical to the petrol version as far as oil changing is concerned and follows the same procedure.

☐ **Job 24. Replace diesel engine oil filter.**

OPTIONAL: This job is specified by Peugeot at 5,000 miles with no time limit specified, but as above, we include it here.

Refer to *Job 42* later in this chapter for precise instructions - the diesel engine is identical to the petrol version as far as oil-filter changing is concerned and follows the same procedure.

25A.

☐ Job 25. Check brake and fuel lines.

SAFETY FIRST! AND SPECIALIST SERVICE
Fuel injection systems remain pressurised even when the engine is switched off and this requires a special procedure to make it safe - UNDER NO CIRCUMSTANCES loosen or remove fuel pipes on a fuel injection system. If pipework requires repair, take the car immediately to a fuel injection specialist or Peugeot dealer.

25A. Make a physical check of all the pipework and connections in the engine bay. Bend the flexible fuel lines in order to expose hairline cracks or deterioration which may not be immediately obvious. Start the engine and check that there are no fuel leaks.

25B.

25B. Look for signs of rust or tell-tale fluid marks on brake pipes and unions - have an assistant apply full pressure to the brake pedal while this check is made.

SAFETY FIRST!
As everyone is aware, petrol is highly flammable and only a small spark is necessary to ignite it, with potentially disastrous consequences. If a fuel leak, (however slight) is suspected or detected; don't smoke, switch off all car accessories (but don't disconnect the battery which often creates sparks as the terminals are removed) and mop-up any spilt or dripping fuel with rags which should be taken immediately out of doors. Don't drive the car until professional advice is sought and the problem rectified.

26A.

☐ Job 26. Check air filter.

Check the air cleaner element for signs of clogging, oil contamination and general condition. Renew it if necessary as follows:

PETROL ENGINES

Refer to **Page 20, Engine Layouts**, for details of your particular model - typical examples follow:

'TU' TYPE ENGINES

26A. The air filter housing on these models is located vertically at the back of the engine. First disconnect the air ducting from the carburettor by loosening the screw shown.

26B.

26B. Disconnect the breather hose from the valve cover (A), and the vacuum hose from the carburettor (B). Note: This is *not* the pipe above, held on with a jubilee clip.

26C. Release the spring clips retaining the top cover, and lift the cover and element from the housing.

26C

DIESEL ENGINES

26D. The air cleaner is located vertically at the front right-hand side of the engine bay. Disconnect the air ducting from the tube on the front panel after undoing the large jubilee clip, remove the screw in the centre of the top cover and lift the cover away allowing the element to be removed.

Every 3,000 Miles - Around the Car

☐ **Job 27. Check wheel bolts.**

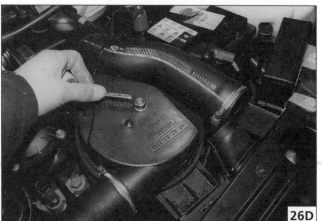
26D

27. Check the tightness of all wheel bolts. The wheel brace supplied with the car is merely intended for use in an emergency and we strongly recommend the use of a torque wrench for this job. This will avoid over-tightening the nuts and avoids the danger of stripped threads or over-stressed bolts.

To 'torque' the wheel nuts correctly, first slacken each nut and check that the threads aren't stiff or corroded - clean off if necessary, then tighten with the wrench to a torque of 85 Nm. (65 lb.ft).

☐ **Job 28. Check handbrake adjustment.**

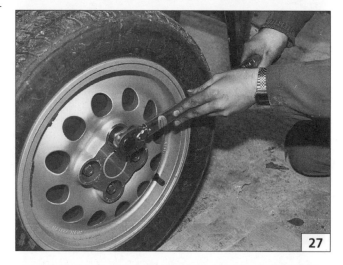
27

SAFETY FIRST!
Don't work beneath a vehicle supported only on axle stands with someone else sitting inside trying the handbrake. It's too risky that their movements will cause the vehicle to fall off the axle stands. Make sure that you are well clear of the raised vehicle when someone is inside it. Read carefully the information at the start of this chapter on lifting and supporting the vehicle.

28. Apply the handbrake, without pressing the release knob at the end of the lever, and count the number of 'clicks' the lever goes through before the brake is firmly applied: the brake should lock at between 5 and 8 clicks. If more or less than these figures, the cable can be adjusted as described in *Job 105*.

Raise the rear of the vehicle sufficiently to allow the rear wheels to turn and to provide sufficient working clearance, and support the body on axle stands. Fully release the handbrake and apply the footbrake firmly several times to ensure the automatic adjusters on each wheel are fully 'set' and the shoes centralised in the drums.

28

☐ Job 29. Check ABS warning light.

29. On models with Anti-lock Braking Systems (ABS) check the operation of the warning light on the instrument panel, which should illuminate for approximately 60 seconds after switching on the ignition. If the light fails to illuminate, or stays illuminated for longer periods, have the system checked by a Peugeot dealer or other reputable garage.

☐ Job 30. Check windscreen.

Check the windscreen for chips and scratches which are a potential MoT test failure point depending on their location and size - see *Chapter 7, Getting Through the MoT*, for what is and is not acceptable according to UK regulations. Most small chips less than 10mm wide can be repaired by specialists, while light scoring can often be polished out by the same firms.

☐ Job 31. Clean and lubricate aerial.

31. Clean each section of an extending aerial with spray lubricant on a cloth and work the aerial up and down a few times. Do not leave excess lubricant on the aerial sections as this will simply encourage the adherence of grit and dirt.

INSIDE INFORMATION: With electrically operated aerials it is especially important to keep the sections clean, otherwise the operating motor and/or gears will be over-stressed and quickly fail.

Every 3,000 Miles - Under the Car

☐ Job 32. Check exhaust system and mountings.

> *SAFETY FIRST!*
> *Never run your car's engine in an enclosed space, only ever out of doors. Exhaust gases can be toxic and an exhaust leak can allow gases into the car as you drive along. Check the condition and security of the entire exhaust system, looking carefully for any signs of corrosion on the pipes and silencers, or leakage at the joints. Replace gaskets if necessary.*

32A. Examine the silencers (as far as safe access will allow) for signs of corrosion, especially along seams and at the ends where the pipes are welded or clamped, on some models. Check the system joints where the pipe sections are joined together for tell-tale 'soot' marks indicating a leak.

32B. If exhaust system mountings break, perish or come loose, the extra stresses on the exhaust system could cause the pipes or silencers to fracture. Always replace worn or damaged mountings before they break - it can save much hassle and expense later on.

making it easy! As well as a visual test, check the mountings by grasping the (cold) exhaust tailpipe with a piece of rag and 'shaking' it, listening for any rattles or bumps that indicate it is contacting the under-side of the car - usually the result of weak or damaged mountings.

☐ Job 33. Check brake and fuel lines.

33A. Carefully examine all the pipes under the car for signs of rust or weeping unions. Deep pitting indicates severe rusting and this, or even the slightest of leaks can render the car dangerous to drive. It must not be driven until the problem has been rectified. Also check the pipes are held securely in their clips, and that there is no physical damage to the pipes from incorrectly placed jacks or as a result of driving over obstacles and flattening the pipes.

33B. Bend all flexible hoses to show up signs of cracking rubber if any are found, the hose should be replaced as soon as possible. The hoses should also be free from bulges or chafing marks.

INSIDE INFORMATION: Bend the hoses double (wherever possible), and check visually near the union ends for any signs of wear or damage. Also, have an assistant press hard on the brake pedal while the hoses are checked for bulging. Any hose not in perfect condition should be replaced as soon as possible.

☐ Job 34. Check steering rack gaiters.

34A. The steering rack gaiters (arrowed) - also sometimes called 'boots' - are made of convoluted rubber, their purpose being to prevent dirt and grit getting inside the steering rack mechanism while keeping the lubricant inside it, and at the same time allowing the 'push-pull' motion of the steering arms as the steering wheel is turned. The 'Identification Label' identifies the correct model of steering rack when replacement is needed. (Illustration, courtesy Peugeot Talbot Motor Co Plc)

After a few years of continual movement plus attack from stones, grit and other road dirt, the gaiter can split leading to dirt and water ingress, which will quickly ruin the rack mechanism. Normally a split gaiter will allow grease or oil to leak out, indicated by a tell-tale oily 'mess' on the exterior surfaces.

34B. The gaiters (there are two, left and right-hand) are located on the bulkhead behind the lower half of the engine. This one is on the driver's side of the car, viewed from beneath the wheel arch. With the steering turned on full lock (turned fully to the left or right) check the gaiter when fully 'open', looking for splits, chafing or perishing. Now turn the steering fully in the opposite direction and check the other gaiter in the same way.

34C. Make sure the gaiter securing clips are secure and doing their job. Clips can be metal bands either sprung or twisted into position, metal clips, or plastic bands commonly known as 'cable-ties'.

33A

33B

SAFETY FIRST!
*This operation requires the steering to be moved from lock-to-lock so the use of axle stands is essential. Refer to **Raising the Car Safely**, at the beginning of this chapter for details of how to do this.*

IDENTIFICATION LABEL

34A

34B

34C

34D

34E

35A

35B

If one or both of the gaiters are defective, replace them as follows:

INSIDE INFORMATION: Renewing a steering rack gaiter isn't a particularly difficult job, but it does call for a special tool - viz. a 'ball-joint separator', and for the 'tracking' of the front wheels to be checked professionally afterwards - a **SPECIALIST SERVICE** *job.*

First slacken the bolts of the wheel nearest the defective gaiter, before raising and supporting the front of the vehicle - see **Raising the Car Safely** at the start of this chapter for details of how to do this safely. Remove the wheel completely.

Remove the track-rod-end as described in *Job 72*.

34D. The clips securing each end of the gaiter can now be removed, the small outer clip of the type shown can be released with pliers and removed.

34E. The gaiter can now be slid-off along the steering arm, and a new one slipped into place. Note: no lubrication of the exposed parts of the 'rack is necessary.

Fit new clips, which should be supplied with the new gaiter. Replace the track-rod-end, fit the wheel and lower the vehicle to the ground, finally tightening the wheel-bolts.

IMPORTANT: The steering 'track' will need to be checked by a specialist, otherwise poor steering response and rapid tyre wear can result.

☐ Job 35. Check drive shaft gaiters.

35A. Check the inner and outer drive shaft gaiters (A and B in the photo). Check for condition of the rubber and for security of the fastenings at each end. Make sure there are no splits, pinholes or signs of chafing; any of these, or any traces of grease leaking from the gaiter requires further investigation and probably replacement.

35B. Check both driveshafts similarly, but note that as the outer joints are subject to a greater range of movement than the inner gaiters, wear is more common. Put the steering on full lock in each direction while each gaiter is checked, so that the rubber is 'stretched' and any weakness or leak will be easier to spot.

35C. This is an example of a gaiter that has split - the grease from the joint is leaking onto the surrounding rubber, and has been thrown onto the brake and suspension components. In this case the split is small and therefore little grime or grit would have found its way into the joint, so early renewal of the gaiter will probably save it.

SPECIALIST SERVICE: If there is any doubt as to the condition of the gaiters, or if they are obviously in need of replacement, consult your Peugeot dealer for advice, as a number of special tools and equipment is required to change them.

☐ Job 36. Check underside of car for leaks.

Check along the car for any signs of fluid or oil leaks. Oil leaks are likely to come from the engine area and are probably a matter of gaskets or oil seals needing renewing. They should be cured because, apart from costing you a lot of money in oil, they make a mess on your garage floor and, if they are allowed to develop, could cause low oil level with possible bearing failure. Some leaks are simple to cure, others not so simple. Decide, with the help of a workshop manual, if you feel competent to tackle any leaks you find. If not, seek early SPECIALIST SERVICE.

FACT FILE: EMERGENCY GAITER REPAIR

35D. There are a number of 'easy-fit' gaiter replacement kits on the market, their main purpose being to enable the gaiter to be renewed without special tools or any dismantling.

35E. These gaiters are split longitudinally, which allows them to be simply placed over the joint, and then joined and sealed with a special cyanoacrylate glue. Fitting this type of gaiter successfully relies on absolute cleanliness as oil or grease will prevent the adhesive setting properly. Full instructions are supplied with each kit. (Illustration, courtesy Partco.)

☐ Job 37. Clean mud traps.

37. Use a strong water jet to clean away any build-up of mud and silt on the underside of the car, particularly the corners and extremities of the wheel arches.

Every 3,000 Miles - Road Test

☐ Job 38. Clean controls.

The door handles, steering wheel, switches and gear lever knob may well have become greasy from handling while you were carrying out the service. Clean them with a rag moistened in hot water containing a little detergent.

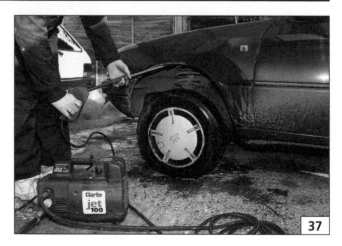

☐ Job 39. Check instruments and controls.

Switch on the ignition while sitting in the driving seat and check that all the warning lights which should come on, do come on. Warning lights which do not work are useless as warnings! Non-functioning may be just a case of a blown bulb, but it may be a symptom of deeper electrical trouble. If changing a bulb does not cure the problem, or if the warning lights fail to go out when they should, seek SPECIALIST SERVICE from an auto. electrician. Check that all the switches are secure and working.

making it easy! Sometimes, because the oil from a leak tends to spread, it is difficult to spot exactly where the leak is coming from. One way of finding it is top clean everything off with a de-greasing agent, dry it, then dust along the joint with talcum powder. When the engine is subsequently run, an oil leak will quickly show-up as a stain on the powder.

Job 40. Check throttle action.

40A. Operate the throttle pedal several times to check that it is smooth over its complete travel. A throttle pedal which is stiff or, worse still, which sticks, can be dangerous as well as making driving a misery. Apply a little oil to the pedal pivots arrowed. If your car has a manual choke control check the smoothness of operation of the choke knob.

40B. INSIDE INFORMATION: If neither throttle (A) nor choke (B) are as smooth as they should be, check that the inner cable isn't fraying where it comes out of the outer casing. Also check the route of the cables to make sure there are no sharp bends or kinks. Later throttle cables with a nylon inner sleeve are much smoother in operation that the older steel sleeve sort. If the fault for a jerky or stiff throttle pedal or choke knob is not the cable, check the linkage at the carburettor for stiffness and lubricate if necessary.

40A

Job 41. Check clutch action.

Operate the clutch pedal several times with the engine switched off; the action of the pedal should be smooth, once the initial take-up of the clutch mechanism occurs - this can be felt as a resistance to the pedal after the first inch or so of movement. Repeat the test with the engine running and listen for any whine or 'scrubbing' noise from the gearbox area when depressing the pedal, which can indicate a worn clutch release bearing, or possible problem with the clutch plate itself.

40B

41A. If the pedal action feels jerky, 'dry' or heavy, first try lubricating the pivots, located at the top of the pedal, and also the pivot at the clutch/gearbox as shown (arrowed), with Castrol DWF or Everyman light oil (see *Job 49.*). (Not all 205 clutch/gearboxes look like this: numerous different types were fitted but the principle remains the same.) If the fault persists then the clutch cable can be suspected - the usual cause is fraying of the inner 'stranded' cable causing it to bind in the outer sheath (arrowed). The solution is replacement of the cable. (Illustration, courtesy Peugeot Talbot Motor Co Plc)

41B. INSIDE INFORMATION: Replacing the clutch cable isn't a particularly difficult job in theory, but in practice the restricted working area in the upper reaches of the footwell, coupled with the need to use two hands (preferably three!) to manipulate the cable and automatic adjusting mechanism makes this an awkward and often frustrating job for the inexperienced! Don't forget - if you start the job but can't finish it, the car will be undriveable and could involve a costly tow-in charge to the nearest garage. Unless you are experienced or live next door to an understanding mechanic, seek SPECIALIST SERVICE for this item.

2CJ01
41A

Job 42. Road test: brakes and steering.

SAFETY FIRST!
Carry out the following tests only in daylight, in clear, dry conditions. Choose a quiet road when there are no other road users or pedestrians about. Use your mirrors to make sure there are no other vehicles following you before carrying out brake tests.

Only a proper brake tester at an MoT testing station can check the operation of the brakes accurately enough for the MoT test, but you can rule out some of the most obvious braking problems on a short road test in the following way. Always check the

41B

brakes at low speed first, before attempting to brake from higher speeds. Drive at about 20 mph, dip the clutch and, with your hands only lightly gripping the wheel, try braking first gently, then harder, though there is no need to do an 'emergency' stop. Ideally, the car should pull up in a perfectly straight line. If the steering wheel kicks in your fingers, if there are any 'clonks' or other noises from underneath, if the car drifts heavily to one side as you brake, or if the brake pedal does not feel firm in operation, drive home very slowly and carefully to investigate further.

If all seems well, repeat the braking tests from a higher speed, say about 40 mph. Again, the car should, ideally, pull up in a straight line. If it drifts just gently to the left when you are on the nearside of the road, this may be due to road camber. Try to repeat the test on a non-cambered stretch of road or find a one-way street where you can try on the other side of the road to see if opposite camber has the same effect.

Check that the steering feels positive, does not kick back unduly over rough surfaces and that the car runs in a straight line when you are holding the steering wheel only lightly. Again, slight drifting may be due to road camber, but more persistent drifting needs investigating. Check that the steering self-centres when accelerating out of both left and right hand turns and, if you can find a suitably deserted stretch of road, pull the car from side to side to see that it straightens itself up. This check can be carried out at quite low speed, 15 to 20 mph is sufficient to show up any faults.

Braking and steering are a vital part of a car's safety. If you find any faults, or even if you are uneasy about anything, seek **SPECIALIST SERVICE** before you carry on using the car.

☐ Job 43. Check C.V. joints for noise (part of road test).

Before concluding the 'road' test (a deserted car park is more suitable for this check), put the car through a series of left and right-hand turns with the steering on full-lock, and listen for any knocking or deep 'clunks' from the front of the vehicle, especially under slight acceleration. Any such noise can indicate wear in the driveshaft constant-velocity (C.V.) joints - have them checked professionally by a reputable garage and don't delay having the joints replaced if defective.

☐ Job 44. Check automatic transmission fluid.

Check the automatic transmission fluid level only after the car has been run, so that the fluid is at operating temperature, and keep the engine running and the handbrake applied throughout the check. Move the gear selector through the various gears several times to fully distribute the fluid in the gearbox internals.

44. With the selector in 'PARK' or 'P' position, lift out the fluid dipstick (A), wipe it clean, reinsert it and withdraw again - check the fluid level which should be between the MIN and MAX marks at the bottom of the stick. See page 47.

Topping-up is carried out by carefully pouring fluid through the dipstick tube - most transmission fluid comes in bottles with a small spout for this purpose. (Illustration, courtesy Peugeot Talbot Motor Co Plc)

Every 6,000 Miles - or Every Six Months, whichever comes first

Every 6,000 miles - The Engine Bay

First carry out Jobs 1 to 5 and 25 to 28.

☐ Job 45. Change engine oil and filter.

Probably the one service operation on which most DIY motorists will 'cut their teeth' is an engine oil change - that is emptying the old oil out through the sump drain plug situated beneath the engine and, eventually, pouring in a specified quantity of new oil through the oil filler, found on the valve cover at the top of the engine. And no matter how technically complex the engine, an oil change still remains basically a simple operation.

45A. INSIDE INFORMATION. Some models are fitted with this type of sump plug, which requires a special square 'key' to remove it - while others will have a simple bolt-headed plug; make sure you have the correct tool before you start.

SAFETY FIRST!

*Refer to the section on ENGINE OILS in **Chapter 1, Safety First**, before carrying out the following work. It is essential to wear rubber or plastic gloves since used engine oil can be carcinogenic. Oil drain plugs are often so tight that they seem to have been fitted by a gorilla with toothache. i) Take care that the spanner does not slip causing injury to the hand or head. (Use a socket or ring spanner - never an open-ended spanner with as little offset as possible so that the spanner is near to the line of the bolt.) ii) Ensure that your spanner is positioned so that you pull downwards if at all possible. Take great care that the effort needed to undo the drain plug does not cause the vehicle to fall on you or slide off the ramps - remember those wheel chocks. iii) Refer to information at the start of this Chapter on Raising a Car Safely.*

making it easy! Apart from small differences in location of the oil filter and the sump drain plug, the procedure is the same for all models. Before draining the sump, run the engine (if cold) for around five minutes to warm the oil slightly, so that it will drain more freely - but not so hot that it will scald. Use an oil drainage container to catch the oil as it drains from the sump - note that the oil will fall in an arc away from the drain hole, so position the container to allow for this. Spread newspaper on the floor beneath the engine bay to protect it from oil spills and drips.

45B. This is the position of the drain plug on engines with the flat 'tea tray' type of sump (arrowed). (Illustration, courtesy Peugeot Talbot Motor Co Plc)

45C. This is the location of the oil drain plug on the great majority of engines - on the TU type engine the plug is slightly further back and placed at an angle - viewed from under the car. As we stated previously, the plug will often be tight and require some force to move initially, when it may suddenly 'give' and offer little or no resistance - be careful not to rap your knuckles! Rubber or plastic gloves can compromise your grip on the spanner, so it may be wise to leave them off for the initial 'tug', but remember to don them immediately the plug has been slackened and before removing the plug completely, as some oil will inevitably spill onto your hands.

45D. Once the plug has started to move in its thread it can be undone with the (gloved) fingers; remember to hold onto the plug when fully unscrewed.

45E. Be ready to reposition your bowl - the angle of 'spurt' changes as the oil flows out of the sump! Allow at least ten minutes for the oil to drain completely.

45F. Remember to replace the drain plug once the oil has FULLY drained, and use a new copper or nylon washer which you can buy from the accessory shop or garage where you bought your oil. Buy it at the same time, then you won't forget it.

FILTER RENEWAL

45G. In all cases the oil filter is the familiar screw-on, throw-away thin metal cartridge type and can be reached either from above or from underneath the car depending on model.

making it easy! It isn't necessary to use excessive force when refitting the sump plug. Simply grip the spanner so that the thumb rests on the spanner head, thereby limiting the amount of leverage that can be applied; use 'firm' pressure only. Before refitting the plug, wipe around the drain hole with a piece of clean cloth to remove any dirt, and check that the sealing washer is fitted.

The easiest way to remove this type of filter is with a strap or chain wrench similar to that shown, which you can buy from any accessory shop.

45H. On XV, XW and XY engines the filter (arrowed) is positioned on the upper side of the crankcase in the engine bay - as the filter faces downwards this means a quantity of oil will be lost when the filter is unscrewed, so place absorbent rags around the filter base before removal to prevent oil spilling over the engine. (Illustration, courtesy Peugeot Talbot Motor Co Plc)

SAFETY FIRST!
DON'T pour the old oil down the drain - it's both illegal and irresponsible. Your local council waste disposal site will have special facilities for disposing of it safely. Moreover, don't mix anything else with it, as this will prevent it from being recycled.

45I. On XU, TU and diesel engine types the filter (arrowed) is in the more conventional position - screwed horizontally to the front of the crankcase, just behind the radiator. On some models it is easier to remove the filter from below, with the car secured on ramps or axle stands.

45J. One full turn of the filter using the wrench is usually enough to get it started, after which it can be unscrewed by hand.

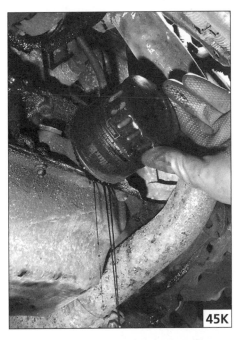

45K. Note that some oil loss will occur, so position an oil tray or container under the engine to catch it. It's also a good idea to place a cloth round the filter when unscrewing it to prevent the oil dribbling over your (gloved!) hand and down your arm! Clean the filter sealing face on the engine with a clean rag.

45L. Make sure the rubber sealing ring is properly fitted to the new filter, then apply a smear of clean engine oil to the ring to prevent it buckling as the filter is screwed home.

45M. Screw the new filter onto the threaded stub, taking care to avoid cross-threading. Most filters have tightening instructions printed in the casing, but essentially all filters are fitted by screwing on by hand only. When the sealing ring contacts the face on the engine, tighten it a further three-quarters of a turn and leave it - there's no need to tighten it any further as this will only distort the sealing ring, cause a leak and make it difficult to remove the filter next time.

45N. Lower the car to the ground, and pour in fresh oil gradually so as not to get a sudden air lock in the valve cover which can make the oil spurt out over the top. Use a funnel to prevent spillages. Dip the level occasionally (1), allowing time for the oil to drain down into the sump. After filling, run the engine for a few minutes to allow the oil to circulate and to fill the filter. Switch off and dip the level again, finally topping up if necessary. Check underneath the car, especially in the areas of the sump plug and filter, making sure there are no oil leaks. On most engines, the filler is in the rocker cover; on this one, it's in an extension tube (2). (Illustration, courtesy Peugeot Talbot Motor Co Plc)

☐ **Job 46. Clean and check spark plugs.**

PETROL ENGINES ONLY

making it easy! 46A. Mark each plug lead with a spot of paint - typists' correction fluid is used by many mechanics as it is easy to apply and dries very quickly. Mark them from the drivebelt-end of the engine in the sequence one, two, three and four 'dots'. (Identification of the plug leads is important as if incorrectly replaced, the engine will not run!).

46A

SAFETY FIRST!
*You may minimise the risk of shock when the engine is running by wearing thick rubber gloves and by NEVER working on the system in damp weather or when standing on damp ground. Read **Chapter 1 Safety First!** before carrying out any work on the ignition system.*

46B. Once this is done the plug caps can be pulled off. Be careful not to tug on the lead itself as you may pull it from the cap, which will remain on the plug!

46B

46C. Using a suitably long spark plug spanner or socket extension, unscrew the spark plugs. They may be 'tight' to begin with so take care to keep the plug spanner or socket in line with the plug body, otherwise the porcelain insulator of the plug can break.

INSIDE INFORMATION: If you are trying to remove a plug which becomes tighter as you turn it, there's every possibility that it is cross-threaded. Once out, it probably won't go back in again. Tighten it up again and take the car to a Peugeot Dealer or specialist who may be able to clean up the threads with a purpose-made tool. If this can't be done, he will have to add a thread insert to your cylinder head. It pays to take great care when removing and fitting spark plugs, especially when dealing with aluminium cylinder heads!

46C

46D. Clean the plug electrodes by vigorous use of a brass-bristled wire brush to remove any carbon deposits. If the electrodes of the plug look 'rounded' and worn (compare them to a new plug) they should be replaced.

46E. If using a flat feeler gauge select the 'blade' of the correct thickness (see *Chapter 8, Facts and Figures*) and slide it between the electrodes as shown. The gap between the two electrodes should provide a sliding fit, with no 'slack'. If necessary, adjust the gap using a pair of snipe-nosed (thin, pointed jaws) pliers, carefully bending the curved side-electrode towards or away from the tip of the centre electrode, until the feeler gauge fits the gap as described.

46D

46E

making it easy! Leave the spark plug in the socket spanner while using the wire brush - this is kinder on the fingers and lessens the risk of dropping the plug and breaking it.

making it easy! 46F. Special gapping tools are available from accessory shops which make this easy and their use carries little risk of damaging the plug, which can occur if the electrode is clumsily moved by use of a screwdriver or pliers.

46G. Replace the plugs when the gaps are correct, adding just a slight smear of copper grease to the threads to make future removal easier. There is no need to screw the plugs down with great force - just tighten them as follows:

Screw each plug in by hand until it is seated. New plugs with flat seats are turned a further 90 degrees with a spark plug wrench. Already used flat-seat plugs, and conical seat plugs, are turned by a further 15 degrees with the wrench.

Job 47. Clean and check ignition components.

47A. Remove each spark-plug HT lead and clean it with a rag. Wipe each lead along its length, from plug cap to the distributor cap. Clean leads one at a time so that their order of fitting is not disturbed.

47B. Unclip the distributor cap (two screws are used on models from 1986) and spray the inner surface with maintenance spray, then wipe clean with a rag.

47C. Clean the distributor cap inside and out and check for any signs of 'tracking' - burnt lines where carbon has lodged in a faint crack to provide a short circuit for the HT current. Any signs of tracking means that the cap could let you down with poor starting and bad running at any time as well as increasing your fuel consumption. Check also that the centre carbon brush still has plenty of length and that it is springy enough to bear on the centre of the rotor arm. Check the studs in the distributor cap for burning. Light burning can be cleaned up with fine glasspaper (better than emery paper because it does not leave any conducting dust behind).

47D. Check that the rotor arm fits firmly and not loosely on the centre cam/spindle of the distributor and check the end of it for burning. Again, light burning can be cleaned up but severe burning of either the cap studs or the rotor arm means renewal.

47E. Clean the coil exterior and check for any signs of HT current tracking. Check that the HT lead, and the low-tension wires, are firm and secure.

47F. This is the 'conventional' coil found on the GTI model - it is located on the right-hand side of the engine bay, as you stand in front of the car.

INSIDE INFORMATION: 1.6 and 1.9 litre engines fitted with a catalytic converter use a 'static' ignition set-up that forms part of the computerised engine management system and as such have no distributor in the conventional sense. However, it is still important to keep the HT leads between spark plugs and ignition module clean - follow the above instructions given in Job 47A.

 If you have to renew either the HT leads or the distributor cap, renew the leads one at a time so you don't get them out of order. With a new cap, compare the position of the connection for number 1 cylinder with the old cap, using the depression where it locates on the body of the distributor as a reference point.

☐ **Job 48. Check water pump.**

XV, XW, XY ENGINES ONLY

The water pump on these models is fitted to the upper left-hand side of the engine block and is turned by the generator drive belt. Check the pump body for signs of leaking - often indicated by a chalky deposit tinged with antifreeze colour, usually light blue or green.

OTHER ENGINE TYPES

On engines other than those described above, the water pump is driven by the camshaft drive belt and the pump is relatively inaccessible. However, as the pump is fitted directly into the engine block, there is less scope for it to leak and problems are few. However, if coolant is seen to be dripping from the rear left-hand corner of the engine have the pump checked by a reputable garage or dealer, after checking all hoses and joints in the vicinity.

☐ **Job 49. Lubricate clutch cable.**

CLUTCH LUBRICATION

Apply a dab of grease to the inner clutch cable where it emerges from the outer sheath, and also to the adjusting screws and locknuts to prevent them rusting. Apply a drop of oil to the intermediate pivot bolt.

CLUTCH ADJUSTMENT

INSIDE INFORMATION: In practice, you will find that clutch adjustment for all models is necessary when the clutch pedal is higher or lower than the brake pedal, i.e. it is correct when the pedals are the same height from the floor.

Adjustment of the early XV, SW and XY engined cars is made by turning the adjuster nut to expand or contract the threaded-rod part of the linkage, positioned between the clutch operating arm and the cranked lever that is connected to the clutch cable.

Adjustment of all other models is made by slackening the 10 mm locknut found on the threaded rod at the end of the clutch cable, and turning the 13 mm nut until the clutch pedal aligns with the brake pedal. It may be necessary to hold the threaded rod with pliers while the nut is turned. Turning the nut (towards the end of the rod) anti-clockwise raises the pedal position, while turning it clockwise lowers it. Before and after adjustment, operate the pedal two or three times to check its position, and ensure the rubber grommets, into which the cable fits at the gearbox, are seated correctly. Finally, tighten the 10 mm locknut up to the 13 mm adjusting nut, without disturbing the position of the latter.

FACT FILE: GEARBOX TYPES

GEARBOXES FITTED TO XV, XW AND XY ENGINES (TYPE BH)
These models are arranged with the gearbox located beneath the engine and the two units 'share' lubrication by way of the engine oil, therefore checking the engine oil level automatically checks that of the gearbox.

XU AND DIESEL ENGINED MODELS UP TO 1989 (TYPE BE1 GEARBOX)
The gearbox on these models has no facility for checking the level between oil changes, which are specified at 36,000 miles. Between these periods (or sooner if preferred) it is wise to check the gearbox casing for oil leaks, particularly around the drive shaft couplings where they emerge from the gearbox, and if necessary seek SPECIALIST SERVICE if leaks are evident.

XU AND DIESEL ENGINED MODELS FROM 1989 (TYPE BE3 GEARBOX)
The combined filler/level plug on this gearbox is situated at the rear of the right-hand end-plate of the gearbox - it is readily accessible from inside the right-hand wheel arch. Check and top-up as for MA type described below.

TU ENGINED MODELS (MA TYPE GEARBOX)
This gearbox type has a combined filler/level plug, and also a drain plug. Although there are no specified times or mileages when the oil should be changed, Peugeot recommend checking the level at 36,000 miles. However, it is wise to check the oil level during this schedule, in case of oil leaks which might otherwise go undetected.
The combined filler/level plug requires a square 'key' to remove it - these tools are available from most accessory shops or your Peugeot dealer.

INSIDE INFORMATION: The car has to be level to obtain an accurate reading, so ramps or axle stands are not suitable; however, the plug can be reached from under the front of the car while it is on the ground or, on certain models, from above, inside the engine bay.

AUTOMATIC TRANSMISSION
The level is checked when the engine is at normal running temperature and WITH the engine running. (Keep hand, hair and clothes away from ignition and electrical components.) With the car on level ground, apply the handbrake and put the gear selector in 'P' (Park). Remove the dipstick, remove with a clean tissue (it's essential to keep dirt off the dipstick and out of the gearbox) and top up if necessary. 'a' on the dipstick indicates the maximum; 'b' the minimum. Readings will be incorrect with the engine cold or stationary. Also see Job 44.

☐ Job 50. Check gearbox oil level.

50A. Remove the plug using the key. The level is correct when oil dribbles from the plug-hole, so if oil is apparent, refit the plug.

50B. If topping-up is required, use the recommended lubricant (see *Recommended Lubricants, page 109*) by inserting the flexible nozzle into the hole and gently squeezing the plastic bottle. Replace the plug when done, to a torque of 25 Nm.

☐ Job 51. Check power steering fluid level (where fitted).

51A. The power steering reservoir is located next to the battery in the engine bay. Clean around the cap before unscrewing it, so that no dirt or grit enters the reservoir which could damage the components.

51B. The cap is fitted with a short dipstick to its underside - the markings relate to the minimum fluid level either when hot (upper mark) or cold (lower mark). If necessary top-up with the recommended fluid (see *Recommended Lubricants, page 109*).

☐ Job 52. Check and turn air cleaner element.

52. Remove the air cleaner top cover (refer to *Job 26* for particular types if different to that shown here) and check the condition of the paper or foam element. Shake it carefully (away from the car!) to remove any loose debris or dust, and check for signs of oil fouling, which could indicate a blocked or defective breather pipe. Clean the filter housing of debris, but be careful not to allow any dirt to enter the open carburettor throat.

Job 53. Lubricate throttle linkage.

Place a dab of grease on the throttle cable where the inner cable exits the outer sleeve at the carburettor linkage, to help prevent water working its way in. Check the cable for any frayed strands or sharp kinks - if present the cable will need to be replaced as there is a danger of the throttle sticking 'open' when least expected.

Job 54. Lubricate carburettor/diesel pump linkages.

54. Apply a few drops of light oil to the carburettor linkages and operating arm, allowing it to soak through the coil springs fitted to the spindles. See *Engine Bay Layouts, drawing 5*.

SAFETY FIRST!
Carburettor adjustment has to be carried out with a warm, running engine. Therefore: i) Watch out for rotating cooling fan and belt and do not wear loose clothing or jewellery and tie back long hair. ii) Take care that you do not burn yourself on the hot engine parts and/or exhaust manifolds. iii) Always work out of doors. DO NOT perform this check in your garage or any confined space - exhaust gases are highly poisonous and can kill within minutes! iv) Apply a strict No Smoking! rule whenever you are servicing your fuel system. Remember, it's not just the petrol that's inflammable, it's the fumes as well. Overall, if you're not (justifiably) confident, give the job to someone who is fully competent. Some manufacturers recommend that only trained mechanics should carry out work on a vehicle's fuel system. Read Chapter 1, Safety First!.

Job 55. Adjust carburettor.

INSIDE INFORMATION: i) This Job requires the use of gas testing equipment and a tachometer to check idle speed, if any meaningful results are to be obtained. Indeed, attempting to 'tune' a carburettor without this equipment is likely to result in increased fuel consumption and poor performance, except in the hands of experienced mechanics although, it has to be said, even they tend to use them anyway, for speed of use and accuracy! ii) The carburettor should be the last part of the engine tune-up procedure, as the general settings will be affected by the condition efficiency of the other engine components such as the ignition system.

First determine which type of carburettor is fitted to your car - see *Chapter 8, Facts and Figures* - then follow the procedure below for that type.

SOLEX 32 & 34 PBISA: WEBER 36 TL

55A. The idle speed (1) and mixture (2) adjusting screws are shown arrowed.

WEBER 32 IBSH and 34 TLP 3

Similar in appearance to the Solex model, the adjusting screws are positioned only slightly differently, the idle screw being horizontal rather than vertical.

SOLEX 35 PBISA and WEBER 35 IBSH

These are twin-choke carburettors - effectively two carburettors side-by-side. Because it is imperative that each 'half' of the carburettor is synchronised correctly with the other before any adjustments are made, take the car to your Peugeot dealer for a SPECIALIST SERVICE if the carburettors require adjustment.

55B. For reference, this is the twin Weber 40DCOM set-up fitted to the 205 Rallye. Setting DCOMs involves i) synchronising the butterflies; ii) balancing the intake vacuum; iii) adjusting mixture: SPECIALIST SERVICE jobs. (Illustration, courtesy Peugeot Talbot Motor Co Plc)

MAKING ADJUSTMENTS - ALL TYPES

ADJUST IDLE SPEED

Adjust the idle screw until the engine is running at the prescribed idle speed, see *Chapter 8, Facts & Figures*. Setting this accurately requires an rpm meter but, if you do not have one, set the engine to run at the slowest speed at which it is comfortable without stalling. Rev the engine to approximately 3,000 rpm for half a minute to clear and stabilise the carburettor and check the idle speed again. The mixture should not need adjusting at this service but, if you cannot get the engine to idle smoothly, the mixture may be inaccurate.

ADJUSTING THE MIXTURE

First connect the exhaust gas analyser according to the manufacturers instructions. The small, recessed, mixture screw on all types of carburettor is turned *anti-*clockwise to richen the mixture, ~~anti-~~clockwise to weaken it. Only a small amount of movement is required to adjust the idle mixture - start by turning the screw a quarter-turn at a time, observing the effect on the gas-tester read-out for each movement of the screw.

☐ Job 56. Check idle speed and mixture.

FUEL INJECTION ENGINES ONLY

INSIDE INFORMATION: An accurate tachometer is essential for this job (even if your model is fitted with a dash-mounted rev. counter as standard), and also an exhaust gas analyser. However, adjustment of either parameter is not recommended for the inexperienced (and is not possible on later models), so whether the expense of this equipment can be justified simply for checking purposes, is questionable - but see Job 57 as a relatively inexpensive option. Your Peugeot dealer is well equipped for the task and the cost reasonable, so you may wish to consider this job a SPECIALIST SERVICE operation.

56A

DIESEL ENGINES ONLY

Idle speed on diesel engines is adjusted by means of a screw on the fuel injection pump. As it is not possible to use the normal electronic tachometer used on petrol engines, the idle speed has to be set 'by ear' to the lowest level that is comfortable for the engine to run without stalling.

56A. The Bosch injector pump is fitted with two screws - be sure to adjust only the one shown here (1), as the other screw governs the maximum engine speed and should not be moved. To adjust, slacken the locknut '2' and turn the screw '1' until the desired idle speed is obtained. Tighten the locknut afterwards. (Illustration, courtesy Peugeot Talbot Motor Co Plc)

56B. The CAV/Roto diesel pump idle adjusting screw is shown at (1), and the locknut at (2). Slacken the locknut adjust, then retighten the locknut.

56B

☐ Job 57. Check exhaust emission.
PETROL ENGINES ONLY

57. Since the introduction of relatively inexpensive test meters for exhaust emissions such as the Gunson one shown here, mixture testing and adjustment has become feasible for home mechanics.

making it easy! Generally, the newer the car the more accurately this can be set, but with older cars it may be necessary to allow an increase in the CO settings to ensure the engine runs smoothly in use. Some trial and error may be necessary to balance the lowest desirable CO reading consistent with smooth running. See *Chapter 7, Getting Through the MoT*, for the maximum allowable CO readings.

Follow the instructions with the meter, remembering to rev the engine between each adjustment of the mixture screw to stabilise the carburettor. However, as it is very easy to cause damage by heavy-handed adjustment of this screw, you may wish to check the exhaust emission and, if the mixture needs adjusting, leave it to SPECIALIST SERVICE. Alternatively, see Jobs 55 and 56.

DIESEL ENGINES ONLY

Petrol emissions meters are NOT suitable for checking diesel exhaust emissions. With a diesel, allow the engine to idle for a few moments and then rev it and hold it at moderately high revs. There may be a puff of black smoke as you first raise the revs but this should clear. If black smoke persists, the injectors may need cleaning. Seek SPECIALIST SERVICE.

57

Job 58. Check pipes and hoses

58. Check all the pipes and hose in the engine compartment, including fuel lines, vacuum pipes, breather pipes, etc. Look for signs of chafing, splitting or perishing of the surfaces, and also check all connections and unions for signs of leaks. Replace any damaged components.

Job 59. Lubricate bonnet release.

59. Apply a few drops of oil to the bonnet release mechanism, dribbling a little through the aperture. Also apply a dab of grease to the cable-end and mechanism from beneath the slam-panel.

Every 6,000 Miles - Around The Car

Job 60. Check seat belts and mountings.

60A. Examine the seat belts for chafing and tug hard at them to check their fixings to the body. With inertia seat belts, check the inertia lock by giving the belt a sharp tug. Fit each seat belt catch into its socket and check that it holds properly and frees easily when the catch is pressed. NEVER try to repair a seat belt or its catch, and do not mix catches and sockets from different belts. If you find anything faulty, replace the whole belt and socket.

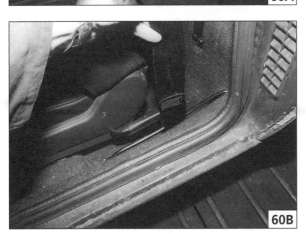

60B. INSIDE INFORMATION: Check the lower belt fixings on three and five door cars and vans, as the belts can be vulnerable damage at this point.

Job 61. Check seat mountings.

61. Check the seats for security by trying to rock them and check the seat adjustment mechanism. Grease the runners lightly and wipe off any surplus to avoid soiling clothes and carpets. Check, if applicable, that the folding seat backs lock securely in the upright position and that the release catches work smoothly.

Job 62. Check fuel filler-cap seal.

Check the sealing rubber on the fuel filler cap to make sure it is not damaged or badly worn. A worn seal here is an MoT failure.

Job 63. Lubricate hinges, locks, check straps.

INSIDE INFORMATION: It doesn't always figure highly, if at all, in service schedules, but there are a fair few moving parts on the motor car which would benefit from occasional oil-can lubrication. They will then work more smoothly, probably more quietly, and will certainly last longer. Here are just a few examples - but if you get into the habit of regularly 'carrying the can' around your car, you'll probably spot a few more!

63A. Door hinges are a prime area of neglect - if the hinges sound or feel 'dry' give them an initial squirt of maintenance spray, followed regularly by a drop or two of thicker oil from a can.

63B. Similarly treat the door check straps, which if left unlubricated dry out and rust up, which not only retards smooth door opening and closing, but also causes those strident 'graunching' noises which are always an embarrassment - particularly in your drive-way late at night! An occasional smear of grease works wonders.

63A

> *making it easy!* On older, or previously neglected door hinges, it could be beneficial to first douse them with penetrating fluid, following up with the oil can a little later, when the penetrating stuff has done its work.

63C. Use a light oil for lubricating stiff lock mechanisms and door lock push-buttons; a drop of oil applied to the lock barrels keeps them working smoothly and helps prevent in cold weather.

63B

63D. Van and hatchback tailgate hinges will benefit from a drop or two of oil as well, as will the tailgate lock and latch. Be careful not to put too much oil on the hinges, as it could seep past the seal and stain the headlining.

☐ Job 64. Check shock absorber action.

Press down on each corner of the car in turn and release your weight. The suspension should 'bounce' back once or twice at the most. If it is easy to compress the springs, and the car 'bounces' several times when you release your weight, the dampers may need renewing - seek **SPECIALIST SERVICE**.

☐ Job 65. Check wheel alignment.

It is important for the front wheels of a car to be properly adjusted, in terms of 'toe-in' or 'toe-out',

63C

63D

often known as 'tracking'. This describes the preset amount of deviation, measured in degrees, of the front wheels from the straight-ahead position. An incorrect setting will affect the handling of the car and also cause the front tyres to wear unevenly - see paragraph 24, *Chapter 7*. This service is quickly and cheaply carried out by most reputable tyre-fitting companies, so is a **SPECIALIST SERVICE**.

Every 6,000 miles - Under the Car

☐ Job 66. Check/renew front brake pads.

SAFETY FIRST!
Raise the front of the car off the ground once again, after reading carefully the information at the start of this chapter on lifting and supporting the car. ii) Obviously, your car's brakes are among its most important safety related items. Do NOT dismantle or attempt to perform any work on the braking system unless you are fully competent to do so. If you have not been trained in this work, but wish to carry it out, we strongly recommend that you have a garage or qualified mechanic check your work before using the car on the road. See also the section on BRAKES AND ASBESTOS in Chapter 1, Safety First! for further information. Always start by washing the brakes with a proprietary brand of brake cleaner - brake drums removed where appropriate - never use compressed air to clean off brake dust. Always replace the brake pads and/or shoes in sets of four never replace the pads/shoes on one wheel only. After fitting new brake shoes or pads, avoid heavy braking - except in an emergency - for the first 150 to 200 miles (250 to 300 km).

66A

66A. You can check the pad thicknesses without removing the caliper. The maker's recommended minimum thickness for the friction material is 2mm but you may want to renew earlier than this because you won't be looking at the pads again for another 6,000 miles. It is normal for one pad to wear slightly more than the other but, if it appears that only one pad is doing all the work while the other has hardly worn at all, it is a sure sign that the caliper is sticking. This means **SPECIALIST SERVICE**. Have the calipers checked by a garage.

making it easy! Wear gloves: brake dust gets in cut and skin cracks and pores and can take ages to 'wear' out!

REPLACING FRONT DISC PADS

ALL MODELS EXCEPT GTI & CTi

66B

66B. First disconnect the pad wear indicator wire at its connector.

66C

66C. The pads are retained by a sliding key, which in turn is retained by this small spring clip - easily removed with pliers.

66D. The sliding pad can then be pulled sideways from between the caliper and the pad ends.

66E. Using a stout screwdriver inserted in this notch, carefully lever the caliper away from the outer pad slightly to allow the pad some clearance...

66D

66E

66F. ...so that it can be lifted away. Slide the caliper towards the suspension leg so that the inner pad can be removed.

66F

66G. Spray on aerosol brake cleaner and thoroughly clean any rust or scale from the calipers using a wire brush - take care not to breathe-in the dust produced.

66H. Apply a light smear of special brake grease (*not* regular lubricating grease!) to the lower pad locating lip on the caliper, and also to the rear face of the pads.

66I. The caliper piston will need to be pushed fully home into its bore - use a large pair of grips like those shown, or a woodworker's G-cramp. Take great care not to damage the rubber bellows. If you do, have a specialist come to you to overhaul the caliper before using the car.

66G

66J. Check the condition of the rubber dust excluder that surrounds the piston; if it is damaged, water and dirt will enter and cause the piston to seize.

making it easy! As the piston is forced into its bore, the brake fluid it displaces will cause the master cylinder reservoir to rise, possibly to the point of overflowing. Raise the bonnet so that the master cylinder can be observed as the piston is pushed home - it may be necessary to syphon a small quantity of fluid from the reservoir, for which purpose an old battery hydrometer is particularly useful to 'suck' fluid from the reservoir.

66H

66I

66J

66K.

66L.

66M.

66N.

66K. If new pads are being fitted, transfer the anti-rattle clips from the old pads to the new, ensuring they are located properly note their orientation before removing.

Fit the inner pad first, then slide the caliper outwards and fit the outer pad. Ensure the lower and upper locating lips of the pads are seated correctly. Position the sliding key between pads and caliper and tap it carefully home with a hammer. Fit the key retaining clip and re-connect the wear indicator wires.

SAFETY FIRST!
Remember that retracting the pistons will produce a gap between the pads and discs that will only be taken up when the brake pedal is depressed a number of times. This means there will be no braking effect for the first few 'pushes' of the pedal, so before lowering the car to the ground make sure the handbrake is fully applied, then get in and firmly push the brake pedal several times to restore the brakes, BEFORE moving off!

1.9 GTI MODELS ONLY

66L. It is strictly only necessary to remove the front caliper retaining bolt for pad replacement, although we recommend both bolts are removed and the caliper and bracket thoroughly cleaned. Steady the caliper-bolt sleeve with a 17mm spanner while the bolt itself is undone. Disconnect the brake wear indicator wires, if fitted to your car.

66M. Swing the caliper AWAY so that the pads can be removed sideways - a sharp tap from a hammer may be needed to free the pads if corroded.

Retract the caliper piston into its bore using a large pair of grips or a woodworker's 'G'-cramp - see *Job 66H.*

Once retracted, check the piston dust excluder for splitting and other damage, which if not rectified may lead to the caliper seizing completely.

66N. Spray on aerosol brake cleaner and scrape any rust or scale from the pad seatings in each end of the bracket with a screwdriver. This is important to ensure free movement of the pads. Also, if the existing pads are to be refitted clean them all over with a wire brush to remove any rust.

Reassemble by fitting the pads to the carrier bracket and replacing the caliper over the pads. Apply a locking compound to the retaining bolts and tighten them to a torque of 35 Nm (25lb/ft).

☐ **Job 67. Check brake discs.**

> *SAFETY FIRST!*
> *If you are in any doubt as to the condition of the disc or discs, seek professional advice. Corroded or pitted areas of the disc's working surface indicates a possible problem with the caliper, which may be partially seized. Additionally, deep scoring causes the pad friction material to contact only the 'peaks' of the ridges, thereby drastically reducing the area of contact, and subsequently reducing braking efficiency.*

67A

67A. Check the disc for signs of excessive corrosion, scoring, uneven wear, and ridges at the inner and outer edges of the pad contact area. Some wear and light scoring is inevitable but if more than a few thousandths-of-an-inch deep then the disc will need renewing.

67B. A ruler has been placed across the disc surface to highlight the ridges present on this particular disc, which in this instance is excessively worn and in need of replacement.

SPECIALIST SERVICE: Consult your Peugeot dealer and have them examine the disc and measure it with a micrometer if deep scoring or excessive wear is suspected.

67B

Badly scored or badly ridged discs will seriously reduce braking efficiency even with fully bedded-in pads. New pads would take for ever to bed-in on them and meanwhile braking efficiency could be virtually nil!

A light ridge, perhaps mostly a build-up of rust, can be carefully removed with a file - it's possible to feed the file (or a hefty old screwdriver) through a pad aperture, then to steady the file (or screwdriver blade) firmly against the ridge while you spin the disc.

> *SAFETY FIRST! AND SPECIALIST SERVICE*
> *Obviously, your car's brakes are among its most important safety related items. Do NOT dismantle or attempt to perform any work on the braking system unless you are fully competent to do so. If you have not been trained in this work, but wish to carry it out, we strongly recommend that you have a garage or qualified mechanic check your work before using the car on the road. See also the section on BRAKES AND ASBESTOS in Chapter 1, Safety First! for further information.*

☐ **Job 68. Check rear brake shoes.**

> *making it easy!* Before dismantling brake shoes, but after the drum has been removed, make a careful record of where everything goes, especially brake shoe return springs. Make a careful sketch, take a couple of photographs (a Polaroid would be ideal) or 'video' the assembly - it could turn out to be a life saver - literally! Also, only work on one side at a time, so that you've always got the other one to refer to. If applicable, refer to the illustration here.

CLEAN AND CHECK CONDITION

If you have bought a used car and are uncertain of its history (service record) then have the rear brakes checked thoroughly by a competent garage or Peugeot dealer as part of the 'clean-sweep' initial service.

VISUAL INSPECTION

Raise the rear of the vehicle and support it on axle stands positioned as described in *Raising the Car Safely* at the beginning of this chapter. Release the handbrake.

68A

68A. The rear of the brake backplate is provided with an inspection hole, covered by a rubber plug, through which the lining thickness can be checked - a small torch is essential to see inside. Looking through the hole, gauge the thickness of the brake lining material.

If the linings are at or near their minimum permissible thickness of one millimetre (1 mm) then they will need replacing, bearing in mind the amount of time before the next service check. This is a **SPECIALIST SERVICE** job - or at least one that you MUST have checked by a specialist before replacing the brake drums if you carry out the work yourself.

making it easy! It is possible to check the brake shoe lining thickness without removing either wheel or drum, using the hole provided on the backplate for this purpose - indeed, on all models this is the manufacturers' prescribed method during normal servicing procedures at intervals of 12,000 miles. However, we recommend this interval is halved to 6,000 miles or six months, unless your car has no obvious faults with the rear brakes in which case, don't wait - act immediately!

SAFETY FIRST!
i) DO NOT be tempted to increase the length (and therefore leverage) of a typical DIY tool in an effort to achieve the necessary force - the tool will most probably bend, or worse, is likely to fracture suddenly and result in damaged bodywork, the car's - or even your own! It is imperative that a new hub nut is fitted on reassembly, tightened to the correct torque (215 Nm or 159 lb./ft.) and staked firmly in place. ii) The force needed to undo the hub nut will cause the rear suspension system to 'rise' as pressure is applied, which can be dangerous if the vehicle is supported on axle stands. The safest way to undo the nut is to remove the wheel and hub nut dust-cover with the rear of the car raised, then refit the wheel and lower it to the ground for the nut to be undone. Once the initial tightness is released, the car can once again be raised and secured on axle stands. Reverse this process when replacing the nut.

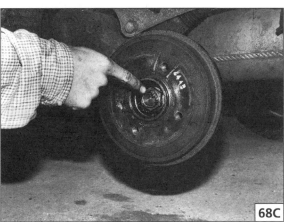

making it easy! A way of helping to distinguish the linings from the steel shoes is to release the handbrake inside the car and then, while looking through the hole, pull on the handbrake cable just adjacent to the rear axle beam, which will cause the shoes to move out towards the drum. In addition, there should be a small 'step' at the joint, which may be more apparent if a thin probe is used to lightly scratch the surfaces. Alternatively, spray a small quantity of brake cleaner into the hole to clean the linings and shoe edges sufficiently to distinguish them.

RENEWING REAR BRAKE SHOES

IMPORTANT NOTE: This is not a job for the inexperience home mechanic! The hub nut is 'staked' to the stub axle by a depression in its outer lip and has to be carefully eased-out using a small chisel, without damaging the threads on the axle-end. Also, the nut itself is tightened to a high torque figure of 215 Nm (159 lb./ft.) when fitted, but with age and use the force needed to unscrew it is considerably greater than this and will require a suitably hefty tool to slacken it, as well as an accurate torque wrench to replace it. For these reasons, if you do not feel confident (or are not properly equipped) to carry out this job regard it as a **SPECIALIST SERVICE** for your Peugeot dealer.

68B. Prise the metal dust cap free. Store it somewhere safe and make sure that it is perfectly clean when you replace it.

68C. After easing-up the indent referred to in the IMPORTANT NOTE earlier...

68D. ...undo the hub-nut using a 32 mm socket and a suitable heavy-duty wrench - in this case a torque wrench is being used 'in reverse'.

68E. Once removed, the brake drum can be pulled free. It may stick on the brake shoes and so you will have to use a screwdriver through one of the wheel stud holes to free the handbrake mechanism.

68F. The washers at either side have to be removed in order to release the assembly. There are strong springs under these washers, so take extra care here.

68G. With a little effort, you should be able to remove the whole of the old brake assembly as one unit. Ease it forward and unclip the handbrake. You'll need long-nosed pliers and preferably a helper to push the spring back.

68H. It is relatively easy to take out the whole assembly as one piece, see here. To the left are the replacement components required for this side. Note that everything, including the cylinder and all washers are springs, is replaced. It's a good idea to lay out the components systematically so that you know exactly where everything goes.

68I. Use a small screwdriver to lift the rear edges of both wheel cylinder rubber dust-excluders (arrowed), checking for signs of fluid leakage, i.e. 'wetness' (but do not confuse this with a small amount of brake grease that may be present). If the cylinder shows the slightest sign of leaking, have it replaced immediately along with the shoes, which are almost certain to have been contaminated by the leaking fluid.

68J. On reassembly use a new nut, tightening it to 215 Nm (159 lb./ft.) with a suitable torque wrench. 'Stake' the nut to the stub axle by placing the side of a screwdriver blade against the thin edge of the nut over the axle's slot, and tapping the blade carefully with a hammer. Ensure the indentation thus made is deep enough to engage with the slot and so prevent the nut from loosening in service.

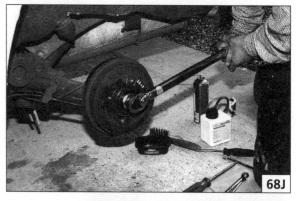

Job 69. Check/renew rear brake pads.

1.9 LITRE GTI MODELS ONLY

REAR PADS - INSPECTION

Slacken the rear wheel bolts before jacking up the car, then make sure it is safely supported - see *Raising the Car Safely* at the beginning of this chapter.

69. With the wheel removed the pads can be inspected through the 'window' in the caliper - a small torch may be useful to see them properly.

INSIDE INFORMATION: Like the front brakes, it is important there is sufficient depth of friction material on the rear pads, which tend to wear at a lesser rate than the front pads. The recommended minimum permissible brake pad thickness is around 7mm (including the steel backing plate) but you should allow for the fact that you won't be checking the brakes again for another 6,000 miles or six months. As brake pads very rarely wear evenly, you should take the thickness of the most worn pad as your guide.

REAR BRAKE PAD REPLACEMENT

The rear caliper is very similar to the front caliper in operation, except for the inclusion of the handbrake mechanism within the caliper which requires a special tool to retract the piston. However, pad replacement is straightforward, but if you are in any doubt as to your abilities or the results of your handiwork, have the brakes checked thoroughly by a reputable garage or Peugeot dealer.

Follow the procedure given above for the front brakes - Job 66 - but note that, due to the nature of the handbrake mechanism, before replacing the caliper it is necessary to 'wind' the piston into its bore using a square-shafted screwdriver acting on the lugs machined into the piston face. Turn the piston clockwise, viewed from the disk side.

☐ Job 70. Check rear brake discs.

Refer to *Job 67* for details and notes on this job.

☐ Job 71. Check brake proportioning valve.

All models have a brake proportioning valve, adjusting brake balance front-to-rear to compensate for varying loads. On vans in particular, it is essential that this valve is set correctly - a **SPECIALIST SERVICE** job.

72A

☐ Job 72. Check steering ball-joints.

CHECK STEERING BALL JOINTS

Steering joints, or 'track-rod-ends' provide the link between the steering arms and the roadwheels. A small rubber boot (arrowed, 72A) covers the steering joint and forms part of the assembly and is vital to the life of the joint - any splits or cracks will allow the grease to escape and dirt to enter and ruin the joint.

It's easier to check the joint if the front wheels are removed first. Refer to *Raising the Car Safely* at the beginning of this Chapter. Put the steering onto full lock so that each joint can be seen at the rear of the brake disc backplate.

72B

72A. Check the condition and security of the protective boot on each track rod end. If split or damaged, the complete track rod end joint will have to be replaced. In theory you can fit a new boot, but it's false economy for the following reasons. i) It is likely that the old joint will be worn due to the split boot allowing the essential lubricant to have been lost or contaminated, and ii), the joint will have to be removed from the steering arm in any case. This can be a difficult job so you might as well fit a relatively inexpensive new joint and have the wheel alignment checked at the same time. (Illustration, courtesy Peugeot Talbot Motor Co Plc)

SPECIALIST SERVICE: This can be a difficult job for the inexperienced mechanic to carry out! A special ball-joint separating tool will be needed and the front wheel 'tracking' professionally adjusted afterwards.

72C

72B. First thoroughly clean around the area of the joint with a wire brush, particularly the threads around the top nut and those that screw into the steering arm.

72C. So that the track-rod-end (TRE) can be replaced in approximately the same position, apply a stripe of white paint (or typist's correction fluid as here) to both the lock-nut and the steering arm.

72D. It is a good idea to soak the threads of the joint with penetrating fluid and leave for a few minutes (or better still - hours!) before slackening the locknut half-a-turn.

72E. Unscrew the top nut, preferably using a ring spanner as shown, and apply plenty of penetrating fluid - see INSIDE INFORMATION below.

INSIDE INFORMATION: These steering joint nuts have a nylon insert that prevents the nut working loose in service - it also makes the nut quite stiff to unscrew, especially as it passes over the exposed threads of the joint which have usually corroded and become 'enlarged' with rust, causing the nut to tighten towards the top of the thread. In these circumstances, a useful tip is to 'work' the spanner from side to side as the nut is gradually undone, which has the effect of clearing much of the corrosion from the threads. In severe cases use a die of the correct thread, or run a scrap nut with a hacksaw cut right through one side of it, down the thread to clear it. This is particularly important for when the nut is replaced, as the threaded pin onto which it fits will not then be held by taper of the joint and will therefore be free to turn, which can make screwing the nut fully home very difficult.

72F. With the nut removed, a special ball-joint-separator tool is required to part the tapered joint. DO NOT be tempted to hammer the top of the threaded pin as this is guaranteed to damage the threads and wreck the joint!

INSIDE INFORMATION: Leave the nut flush with the top of the stud (A) - so the thread can't be damaged - until the tape comes free. (Illustration, courtesy Peugeot Talbot Motor Co Plc)

72G. Position a spanner on the flats at the inner end of the arm as shown and use a strong pair of grips to unscrew the joint. DO NOT allow the arm to rotate as this will affect the wheel tracking dimension and could damage the rack gaiter. If a new joint is to be fitted, count the number of full turns needed to fully unscrew the joint, as a reference for fitting the new one.

Reassemble by screwing on the joint - if a new one is being fitted, wind it in using the same number of turns needed to undo the old one, stopping just short of the lock-nut, which should tighten fully by the half or full-turn with which it was loosened. Fit the tapered pin to its seating and fit the top-nut, tightening it to a torque of 35 Nm (26 lb/ft). Replace the roadwheel.

IMPORTANT NOTE: Now have the track set at your Peugeot dealership or local tyre specialist.

Every 12,000 Miles - or Every Twelve Months, whichever comes first

Every 12,000 Miles - The Engine Bay

First carry out Jobs 1 to 5, 25 to 28, and 49 to 68

73

□ Job 73. Change air cleaner element and clean housing.

Change the air cleaner element, referring to *Job 52* for details.

73. When you lift out the old air cleaner element you may find dirt and dust inside the housing bowl - wipe it clean before fitting the new element. It is normal to find a slight oil mist inside the bowl but, if there is a lot of liquid oil, investigate the valves and filters in the breathing system, see *Job 79.*

□ Job 74. Check and adjust valve clearances.

All Peugeot 205 engines are of Over-Head Camshaft (OHC) design, the XU and Diesel engines using a 'bucket and shim' method for adjusting the valve clearances, which precludes adjustment by the home mechanic and is best left to a Peugeot dealer who will have the necessary equipment and skills to carry out the work properly a **SPECIALIST SERVICE.**

74A

XV, XW, XY AND TU ENGINES ONLY

IMPORTANT: Always check the valve clearances when the engine is COLD, i.e. after standing overnight or at least six hours after running.

Although of OHC design, these engines use valve-operating rockers which are more easily checked and adjusted by the home mechanic, as follows:

First remove the HT leads from the spark plugs, followed by the plugs themselves. On XV, XW and XY engines remove the oil filler/ventilation cap from the rocker cover: On TU engines removed the breather pipe from the rocker cover to the air cleaner housing.

74A. Undo the two nuts ('A' in the drawing) and lift off the cover (1); beneath it will be found two spacers (B) and a deflector plate (C) which are lifted away to expose the valve rockers. Always fit a new gasket (D). (Illustration, courtesy Peugeot Talbot Motor Co Plc)

CHECKING ORDER

74B

74B. Using a spanner on the crankshaft pulley bolt (arrowed), turn the engine (clockwise, looking at the pulley) until the rockers on valves 1 and 2 are 'rocking'; that is, when the two valves are moving in opposition with one just closing and the other just opening. Note that number one cylinder is that nearest the gearbox end of the engine, and that the cylinders and valves number out towards the left. Follow the sequence below - inlet valves are marked 'In' and exhaust valves 'Ex'. (Illustration, courtesy Peugeot Talbot Motor Co Plc)

XV, XW, XY ENGINES

Valve Clearances - Inlet 0.10mm: Exhaust 0.25mm

VALVES ROCKING	VALVES TO ADJUST
1 In - 2 Ex	7 In - 8 Ex
5 In - 6 Ex	3 In - 4 Ex
7 In - 8 Ex	1 In - 2 Ex
3 In - 4 Ex	5 In - 6 Ex

TU ENGINES ONLY

Valve Clearances - Inlet 0.20mm: Exhaust 0.40mm.

A different sequence applies to this engine, in that two valves are checked/adjusted while one valve is open, that is, when fully depressed by the rocker arm. Note that the exhaust valves are at the front of the cylinders, the inlets at the rear; No1 cylinder is at the gearbox end of the engine.

VALVE FULLY OPEN	ADJUST VALVES
No 1 Ex	No 3 In & No 4 Ex
No 3 Ex	No 4 In - No 2 Ex
No 4 Ex	No 2 In - No 1 Ex
No 2 Ex	No 1 In - No 3 Ex

74C. Using the correct size of feeler gauge for the valve being checked, slide the blade between the top of the valve stem and the bottom of the arm-adjuster. The blade should be a sliding fit in the gap, with little or no slackness, but not so tight as to prevent the blade moving freely. (Illustration, courtesy Peugeot Talbot Motor Co Plc)

If adjustment is required, slacken the locknut with a spanner and turn the adjuster screw until the blade is a firm fit, then tighten the locknut while holding the screw in position with the screwdriver. Check the gap afterwards, as it can reduce as the locknut is tightened. When satisfied the gap is correct, rotate the engine using a spanner on the crankshaft pulley bolt (see **74B**), to the next step of the given sequence.

Before re-fitting the valve cover, check the gasket or rubber seal fitted to its bottom edge is in good condition, otherwise replace it.

☐ Job 75. Check ignition timing.

NOT DIESEL, OR PETROL MODELS WITH CATALYST

75A. INSIDE INFORMATION: To check or adjust the ignition timing to the required degree of accuracy calls for the use of a stroboscopic timing light similar to the Gunson's model shown here. Although a 'static' timing figure may be given in some workshop manuals, this is only a guide, mostly used to get an engine started after the distributor has been disturbed and the previous settings lost.

75B. The timing marks are located on the flywheel and viewed through the gearbox casing 'window' after pulling off a plastic cover via the tab (arrowed). The window is positioned towards the front of the casing, between engine and radiator, adjacent to the engine number identification plate. On TU engines it is necessary to remove the hot air ducting between the exhaust heat shield and the air cleaner duct, in order to see the window.

 *Turn the engine by hand (i.e. a spanner on the crankshaft pulley bolt - see **74B**) so that the timing mark or 'notch' on the rim of the flywheel can be seen - highlight it with a dab of white paint or typist's correction fluid. This ensures the marks will be clearly visible when illuminated by the timing light. Also, disconnect the small bore pipe from the vacuum capsule on the side of the distributor, and plug the pipe with a wooden bung, screwdriver, or a punch, as shown.*

75C. Connect the timing light in accordance with the manufacturer's instructions (remembering that No. 1 cylinder is at the gearbox end of the engine), make sure there are no wires or other obstructions in the vicinity of the moving parts, start the engine and allow it to idle. Point the flashing timing light beam at the timing marks and observe the position of the 'stationary' flywheel mark in relation to that on the fixed plate.

75D. There are two basic types of fixed timing-mark plate, as shown, but in all cases the correct (10 degree) mark is the first, or upper, mark (arrowed). (Illustration, courtesy Peugeot Talbot Motor Co Plc)

75E. If the timing marks are not correctly aligned, adjustment is carried out by slackening the distributor clamp bolts just sufficiently to allow it to be turned one way or the other. The amount of movement needed is usually quite small; turn the distributor clockwise to advance the timing, anti-clockwise to retard it. (Illustration, courtesy Peugeot Talbot Motor Co Plc)

Once the timing marks are correctly aligned, stop the engine, tighten the distributor clamp bolts and start the engine again, making a final check on the timing mark alignment. If correct, stop the engine, disconnect the timing light and replace the distributor vacuum advance pipe.

Job 76. Check coolant.

76. Check the specific gravity of the antifreeze with a hydrometer. This is similar to the hydrometer for checking battery acid and can be bought at most accessory shops. Follow the instructions and, if the specific gravity is too low, add more antifreeze.

INSIDE INFORMATION: Remember that antifreeze, even in diluted form, will attack paintwork. Be particularly careful when topping-up - any spilt antifreeze should be washed off immediately with plenty of cold water.

Job 77. Check vacuum hoses.

77. Check the security of the vacuum hose from the inlet manifold (vacuum pump on diesel engines - arrowed) to the brake servo. Bend it in your fingers - if it feels brittle, or if you hear any signs of cracking, the hose needs renewing.

Also check the condition and security of the vacuum pipe to the distributor advance and retard capsule, and those to the air cleaner housing temperature flap.

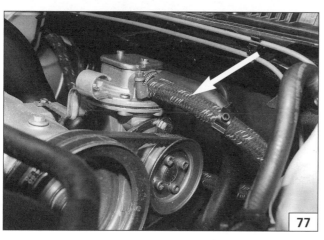

Job 78. Check/renew crankcase emission hoses.

Check the condition and security of all the hoses and clips in the crankcase emission control system. Numerous types and layouts of crankcase emission valves and filters have been fitted to Peugeot engines over the years depending on the type of engine, its capacity and its age. Refer to your workshop manual for full details. Failure of one or more of the devices is often indicated by oil being drawn into the air cleaner housing. If this happens consistently, seek **SPECIALIST SERVICE** to determine which of the valves is at fault as it often needs specialist equipment to check them.

Job 79. Clean oil filler cap.

Clean the oil filler cap with a rag, checking the rubber sealing ring is intact and in good condition, otherwise renew it.

☐ **Job 80. Check air-pump belt.**

DIESEL ENGINES ONLY

80. Check the tension of the air-pump belt by pushing with the thumb, approximately half-way along its length - the belt should deflect by no more than 5mm. Check also the condition of the belt for signs of fraying or splitting, replacing it if necessary following the instructions given in *Job 21*.

☐ **Job 81. Renew spark plugs.**

Change the spark plugs annually - see *Job 46* for detailed instructions.

☐ **Job 82. Clean glow plugs.**

DIESEL ENGINES ONLY

82A. Remove the battery earth lead. Disconnect the electrical lead to the bus bar joining the glow plugs, remove the nuts and washers from the glow plugs and lift away the bus bar.

82B. Unscrew each glow plug in turn with a spanner and clean the carbon from the end with a non-fluffy rag and clean diesel fuel, or a proprietary carburettor cleaner. NOTE: Wear plastic gloves as diesel fuel can cause irritation to the skin and possible dermatitis. After cleaning and replacing the plugs, reconnect the bus bar, the cable and the battery connection. Retighten to the torque figure shown in *Chapter 8, Facts and Figures* or, if you don't own a torque wrench, just enough to compress the sealing washer. Don't undertighten: there could be compression loss. Don't overtighten: you'll strip the thread. A torque wrench is recommended!

☐ **Job 83. Clean/protect battery terminals.**

making it easy! 83. *If the terminals on your battery are showing signs of growing white or green fur or crystals, clean them off by pouring boiling water over the terminals. Dry them off, check the tightness of the connections and coat the terminals with petroleum jelly (Vaseline) to prevent further attack. If they are badly corroded, unbolt, sand them clean and reassemble.*

You can learn a lot about the condition of an engine from looking at the spark plugs. The following information and photographs, reproduced here with grateful thanks to NGK, show you what to look out for.

1. Good Condition

If the firing end of a spark plug is brown or light grey, the condition can be judged to be good and the spark plug is functioning at its best.

4. Overheating

When having been overheated, the insulator tip can become glazed or glossy, and deposits which have accumulated on the insulator tip may have melted. Sometimes these deposits have blistered on the insulator's tip.

6. Abnormal Wear

Abnormal electrode erosion is caused by the effects of corrosion, oxidation, reaction with lead, all resulting in abnormal gap growth.

5. Normal Wear

A worn spark plug not only wastes fuel but also strains the whole ignition system because the expanded gap requires higher voltage. As a result, a worn spark plug will result in damage to the engine itself, and will also increase air pollution. The normal rate of gap growth is usually around 'half-a-thou.' or 0.0006 in. every 5,000 miles (0.01 mm. every 5,000 km.).

7. Breakage

Insulator damage is self-evident and can be caused by rapid heating or cooling of the plug whilst out of the car or by clumsy use of gap setting tools. Burned away electrodes are indicative of an ignition system that is grossly out of adjustment. Do not use the car until this has been put right.

2. Carbon Fouling

Black, dry, sooty deposits, which will eventually cause misfiring and can be caused by an over-rich fuel mixture. Check all carburettor settings, choke operation and air filter cleanliness. Clean plugs vigorously with a brass bristled wire brush.

3. Oil Fouling

Oily, wet-looking deposits. This is particularly prone to causing poor starting and even misfiring. Caused by a severely worn engine but do not confuse with wet plugs removed from the engine when it won't start. If the "wetness" evaporates away, it's not oil fouling.

☐ **Job 84. Check battery specific gravity.**

making it easy! Use a coin to undo cell caps, rather than a screwdriver. The slots are very wide, made of soft plastic and just chew up if you try to use an ordinary screwdriver.

84

84. The strength, or specific gravity, of a battery's electrolyte is the best indication of its state of charge. This is checked using a hydrometer, a simple instrument which you can buy cheaply at most accessory shops. Place the end of the hydrometer into each cell of the battery in turn, squeeze and release the rubber bulb so that a little of the acid is drawn up into the transparent tube. The float, or floats, inside the tube (small coloured beads are sometimes used) give the specific gravity and indicate the state of charge.

INSIDE INFORMATION: If a battery is flat because the car has been left standing for too long, use a small battery charger to recharge the battery, following the maker's instructions and first disconnecting the car's battery. A battery that goes flat too rapidly in use may have one or more cells which are failing. The hydrometer will indicate this by giving a lower reading on the faulty cells after charging. If the hydrometer indicates that all the cells are in good condition, suspect a wiring fault allowing the current to drain away but do be aware that some car alarms will drain a battery in around a week. They are designed primarily for cars that are used almost every day, rather than those that may not be used so often.

☐ **Job 85. Replace fuel filter.**

DIESEL ENGINES ONLY

85A

85A. Earlier models were fitted with a Lucas/CAV filter unit, located in the rear-left corner of the engine bay. Position a container beneath the filter to catch the fuel that is likely to be spilt, and open the drain valve arrowed.

85B. The filter is removed by unscrewing the through-bolt (arrowed). This will allow the lower bowl and the filter element to be lifted clear, and a new element fitted. ALWAYS fit a new element with new seals, wetting them with a little diesel fuel first.

85C. After filter replacement it is necessary to 'bleed' the air from the housing; slacken the bleed screw (A) and unscrew the plunger (B) - work it up-and-down to pump air from the fuel lines and filter housing. Continue pumping until clean fuel issues from the bleed screw (catch it in a piece of rag) then tighten it and return the plunger to its lowered position.

SAFETY FIRST!
i) Whenever you are dealing with diesel fuel, it's essential to protect your hands by wearing plastic gloves. ii)Keep diesel fuel away from the clutch and brakes, the starter motor and any rubber components. Protect tarmac surfaces by putting down newspaper.
IMPORTANT NOTE: Dirt is the enemy of fuel injection systems; even a microscopic quantity can be disastrous. Clean thoroughly around the filter before dismantling and work with clean lint-free rags to wipe every component clean before re-assembling.

85B

85C

12,000 MILE SERVICE

85D. Later models use a different type of filter, positioned to the right of the engine over the gearbox. A disposable-element filter is contained beneath the top cover.

85E. **IMPORTANT NOTE:** Before removing the top cover, drain the filter housing by opening the bleed screw (A) - there should be a plastic tube attached to the housing to allow the fuel to drain away. If this operation is not performed, fuel will run into the clutch mechanism and possibly ruin it. When fully drained, remove the four top-cover screws (B) with an Allen key and lift it to one side. (Illustration, courtesy Peugeot Talbot Motor Co Plc)

85F. Lift out the filter element (C) and clean the bowl beneath it. On fitting the new filter, make sure the sealing ring (D) is fitted correctly around the top of the element before replacing the top cover and tightening the screws. (Illustration, courtesy Peugeot Talbot Motor Co Plc)

85G. The system will now need the air in the filter housing to be 'bled'; do this by closing the bleed screw on the filter housing, and squeezing the rubber hand-pump (B) until fuel can be felt to be passing through it. (Illustration, courtesy Peugeot Talbot Motor Co Plc)

PETROL INJECTION ENGINES

85H. The fuel filter is of the replaceable canister type, located in the left-hand rear corner of the engine bay, adjacent to the brake master cylinder.

SAFETY FIRST!
Disconnect the battery BEFORE carrying out the following work, and only re-connect it after mopping-up any spilt fuel and clearing away any petrol-soaked materials (rags, paper towels etc.). DON'T SMOKE and keep any hot or spark-inducing tools and equipment away from the working area.

Renew the filter by first slackening the clamp screw 'A' to allow the filter to be raised; place a rag beneath the filter to catch any spilt fuel, and undo the top and bottom fuel-pipe unions 'B' carefully noting the position of any washers or seals between union and filter. After lifting out the canister, connect a new one to the two unions, position it in the clamp and tighten. Finally, after referring to the above *SAFETY FIRST!* section, switch on the ignition and check for any fuel leaks around the unions.

INSIDE INFORMATION: It may be necessary to slacken the clamp-mounting nut 'C' in those cases where slackening screw 'A' is insufficient to free the canister.

☐ **Job 86. Fault code readout.**

SPECIALIST SERVICE. Certain models with computer-controlled engine management systems have the ability to store information about the engine and components, which can be 'read' using a fault-code reader. These devices are standard equipment at Peugeot dealers and it is usual to have them read the codes at normal service intervals. Certain

12,000 MILE SERVICE

adjustments to the timing and fuel system are only possible when a code reader is connected, for instance the idle speed and mixture settings.

Code readers have until now been prohibitively expensive for the home user to purchase, but recently Gunson's have introduced a reader for d.i.y. use at a reasonable cost - see *Appendix 2* for their address.

87A

☐ **Job 87. Check tool kit and jack.**

87A. The jack and wheel brace are located in the engine bay, secured to the front-inner left hand wing by a wheel nut. Remove the jack and apply a few drops of light oil to the screw threads and the pivot joints.

87B. The wheel brace is positioned behind the jack, secured by to plastic clips - simply check that it's there: you could be stuck without it!

87B

☐ **Job 88. Check light unit seals.**

88. Check the rubber seals around the rear light clusters for signs of splitting or perishing. Defective seals will allow water to enter the individual light units and possibly corrode the bulb holders, as well as providing an easy path for water to enter the luggage area.

88

☐ **Job 89. Check door/tailgate seals.**

89. Check the rubber door and tailgate seals for damage. Particularly prone to damage (and therefore allowing water leakage into the car) is the lower tailgate seal shown.

☐ **Job 90. Adjust headlight alignment.**

It is possible to adjust your own headlights but not with sufficient accuracy to be safe or within the law. Badly adjusted headlights can be very dangerous if they don't provide you, the driver, with a proper view of the road ahead, or they dazzle oncoming drivers. Older drivers and those with poor eyesight can become disorientated when confronted with maladjusted headlights. **SPECIALIST SERVICE:** Have the work carried out for you by a garage with beam measuring equipment. Any MoT testing station in the UK will be properly equipped.

89

☐ Job 91. Renew wiper blades.

91. Wiper blades don't last for ever, even though some people seem to think they do! It's a good policy to change them every year at least, not only on safety grounds but because a clear screen makes driving, especially at night, so much more comfortable. And don't forget - scratches on a windscreen can result in MoT test failure! Refer to *Job 11* for details of how to change the blades, and also the wiper arms.

☐ Job 92. Check soft-top and frame.

CONVERTIBLES ONLY

92A. Erect the soft top and go carefully over the hood cover looking for signs of rotting stitches. Check the condition of the rear window. If you find anything amiss, it is best to call in the services of a professional car-trimmer as repairing soft tops at home, though possible, is not the easiest of jobs, nor is it assured of success. (Illustration, courtesy Peugeot Talbot Motor Co Plc)

92B. Check the folding action of the frame and lubricate the joints, wiping off excess oil afterwards to avoid soiling clothes or better still, using non staining silicone lubricant. (Illustration, courtesy Peugeot Talbot Motor Co Plc)

☐ Job 93. Check floors.

Lift the carpets and check for signs of rust and wet on the floor underneath. If you find any, deal with it before any leaks are left for so long that you face the problem of seriously rusted metal as well. If you find any wetness, you will probably have to take the seats and the carpets right out to dry the carpets and any underfelt. Tracing leaks isn't the easiest of jobs, and sometimes the only way is to dry the floor thoroughly and then get someone play a hose on the underside of the car, round the doors and over the bonnet while you look inside.

INSIDE INFORMATION: Leaks through spot-welded seams may be just an indication of the original sealant having dried out and crumbled, in which case a new dose of mastic sealant will cure the problem. But it might just be the first sign of something more serious, like rusting. If you are in any doubt about the soundness of any part of the floor pan structure, seek SPECIALIST SERVICE at once. An early professional repair will save you pounds later on as well as ensuring that your car is structurally sound and safe. After any repair or re-sealing, give the inside of the floor pan a coating of mastic such as body underseal. This doesn't normally dry right out but, when it is touch-dry, you can cover it with sheets of polythene to stop the carpets sticking to it.

☐ Job 94. Renew batteries in car alarm sender.

If your car is fitted with a remote control alarm system it is most galling to arrive at the car and find that you cannot get into your own car without setting off the alarm! Don't wait for the batteries to fail; renew them now.

☐ Job 95. Check wiring and terminals.

95. These items are by no means confined to the engine bay of course, but this is where the majority will be found. Terminals hanging by a thread or two could just be a breakdown waiting to happen - or even a fire. Your local accessory shop will stock standard-sized terminals and a crimping tool for fitting them.

☐ Job 96. Clean radiator exterior.

Modern radiators are finely engineered to fit the maximum amount of cooling surfaces into the smallest space, which means the spacing between the cooling 'tubes' or fins of the core are fine and prone to clogging. Dead flies, leaves, litter etc. can drastically reduce the effective cooling area of the radiator, so clean the core by directing a water jet from a garden hose through it - most effectively from the engine-bay side. A high-pressure jet isn't necessary and could damage the cooling fins, so keep the pressure down or use a spray attachment.

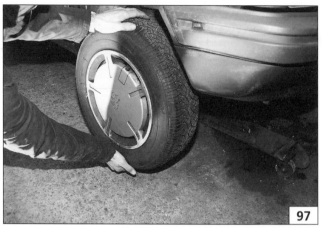

97

Every 12,000 Miles - Under the Car

☐ Job 97. Check wheel bearings.

97. Raise the front of the car just sufficiently for the wheels to be clear of the ground. Grip the top and bottom of the wheel and try to rock it with a push-pull motion, feeling for any sign of slackness or movement. If there is more than just the slightest suspicion of movement, have the wheel bearings checked by **SPECIALIST SERVICE**. Do the same for the rear wheels after releasing the handbrake, and then spin each wheel, listening for any 'rumble' or roughness from the hub (but don't confuse this noise with the 'rubbing' sound commonly caused by the brake pads or shoes contacting the discs or drums slightly).

98A

☐ Job 98. Check steering and suspension.

98A. With the front wheels just clear of the ground, grasp the wheel at the sides and try to turn it from side to side. If you feel free play, put the car up on axle stands and get someone to turn the wheels while you investigate where the free play is occurring. If it is in one of the steering ball joints, these can be renewed, see *Job 72*. If, however, the play is in the steering rack, seek **SPECIALIST SERVICE**.

Test the steering column by grasping the steering wheel and rocking it up-and-down and sideways. Excessive play needs to be investigated - seek professional advice.

98B

98B. With the front wheels still raised just clear of the ground, put a lever under the wheel and try to lever it upwards. If you get any free play it means wear in the suspension bushes or suspension strut. Seek **SPECIALIST ADVICE**.

☐ Job 99. Check steering rack mountings.

99A

99A. Check the bolts securing the steering rack to the bodywork for tightness, using a spanner. (Illustration, courtesy Peugeot Talbot Motor Co Plc)

99B. Power steering assembly bolts should be checked to the following recommended torque settings: the four bolts (9) to 7.5 m.daN (55 lbf ft); two nuts (10) to 5.25 m.daN (39 lbf ft); one bolt (11) to 4.5 m.daN (33 lbf ft).

☐ Job 100. Check front suspension units.

100. Check the front spring/damper units (correctly termed 'Macpherson struts'), looking for badly corroded or broken springs. Make sure the drain holes in the lower spring seat-pan are clean and clear. Check the damper inside the spring for signs of oil staining, indicating a failed unit - have it investigated and always renew dampers in pairs, one each side of the car.

SAFETY FIRST!
The front of the car needs to be raised sufficiently to allow the front suspension components to be checked - see 'Raising the Car' at the beginning of this chapter for details of how to do this safely. Note that it will be necessary to position the axle stands under the chassis so that the suspension is free to 'hang' down, i.e. without bearing any weight.

☐ Job 101. Check front suspension bushes.

101. Check the rubber bushes at each mounting point of the front suspension components, looking for signs of splits, perishing or other damage. Check also the anti-roll bar bushes and the tie-bars. Here, the anti-roll bar link to the strut is being checked for tightness.

☐ Job 102. Check rear springs and shock absorbers.

102. Examine the rear shock absorbers, looking for signs of 'wet' oil-staining which could indicate a leak. Grasp the damper and try to rock it - there should be little or no free play, but if there is, check the mounting bolts and rubber bushes for tightness and condition. Renew if necessary.

INSIDE INFORMATION: The rear suspension arrangement on these cars consists of two torsion bar 'springs' positioned either side of a cross-tube running across the car, therefore any problem such as 'sag' or weakness in the springs will be evidenced by the car appearing to lean to one side - rectification is a SPECIALIST SERVICE job.

SAFETY FIRST!
The rear of the car needs to be raised sufficiently to allow the suspension components to be checked - see 'Raising the Car' at the beginning of this chapter for details of how to do this safely.

☐ Job 103. Check rear suspension bushes.

The design of the rear suspension springing is such that making any visual check is difficult due to the close proximity of each component; however, if any 'clunking' or knocking noises are heard from the rear of the car while driving, have the rear suspension checked by a Peugeot dealer.

☐ Job 104. Check engine and gearbox mountings.

104. Examine the engine mountings for signs of perishing, splits, and cracks in the steel brackets (the mounting shown is located at the rear of the engine, behind the sump). Use a large screwdriver or lever to check that the metal-rubber-metal 'sandwich' doesn't separate when pressure is applied. 'Rock' the engine fore and aft by pushing on the valve/camshaft cover - only a small amount of movement should be evident, otherwise seek SPECIALIST SERVICE.

☐ Job 105. Check/adjust/lubricate handbrake cable.

Check the cable outer sheath along its length for signs of chafing or other damage. Operate the handbrake lever and feel for any roughness in operation that may indicate a damaged or frayed inner cable.

105. The handbrake adjusting mechanism is located inside the car beneath a plastic trim panel, removed by undoing two screws. Raise the rear of the car, support it on axle stands and chock the front wheels. Pull-up the handbrake lever by five clicks and screw-in the compensator adjusting nut as shown, until the wheels can be heard to lightly rub on the brake shoes when turned by hand. Apply the handbrake fully (up to eight clicks) and check that both rear wheels are locked. Make *certain* that the wheels are free to turn with no evidence of one or both wheels 'grabbing' when turned by hand, when the handbrake is let off again. Lower the car to the ground and remove the front wheel chocks.

Apply grease liberally to the handbrake equaliser and oil the cables where they enter the outer cables in the floor. Apply a few drops of oil to the handbrake lever pivots, wiping away any excess.

☐ Job 106. Check underside of body structure.

Examine the underbody structure for corrosion, particularly in the vicinity of welded joints and seams, and also for 'mechanical' damage caused, for instance, by driving over high kerbstones. Make good any damage to the underseal coating using a wax-based product.

☐ Job 107. Clear drainage holes.

107. Check and clear drainage holes in door bottoms, sills, boot/luggage area etc. Use a thin probe to poke the holes clear, while for a lasting job a vacuum cleaner and nozzle will clear most debris. Check also the nooks and crannies around the bulkhead at the rear of the engine bay, especially for leaves in autumn and winter - your vacuum cleaner is possibly the only thing that will shift them!

☐ Job 108. Renew brake fluid.

SPECIALIST SERVICE: Peugeot recommend that brake fluid is changed annually on all models of all ages of their cars. This is best carried out by a reputable garage or Peugeot dealer, who will have the necessary facilities to carry out the work thoroughly and safely.

Every 24,000 Miles - or Every Two Years, whichever comes first

109A

109B

☐ **Job 109. Replace coolant and clean expansion tank.**

109A. The radiator drain plug is located on the lower-left side of the radiator (as you look into the engine bay). Position a container beneath, remove the coolant filler cap and unscrew the drain plug. On those cars fitted with a bottle-shaped coolant header-tank, unclip and lift the tank to allow it to empty completely.

109B. Where there is a drain plug in the radiator block, remove that as well. (Illustration, courtesy Peugeot Talbot Motor Co Plc)

making it easy! *109C. Clean the insides of the tank with a long-handled brush and a little detergent, flushing through with clean water.*

MODELS WITH 'BOTTLE' -TYPE EXPANSION TANK:

109D. After refitting the drain plugs, re-filling is carried out by unscrewing the radiator filler cap located in the front bonnet slam-panel, and adding a 50/50 mixture of antifreeze/summer coolant and clean water. INSIDE INFORMATION: a spark plug spanner is a good fit for the radiator filler cap!

109E. A bleed valve is fitted to the heater return hose which allows air trapped in the cooling system to escape as coolant is added and on non-GTI models, there's one in the inlet manifold coolant hose - unscrew the valves while filling. (Illustration, courtesy Peugeot Talbot Motor Co Plc)

109C

109D

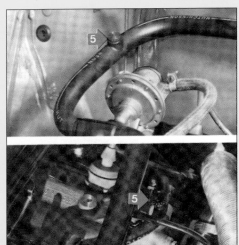

109E

109F. When the radiator is full, release the expansion bottle from its rubber strap and raise it high above the level of the bleed valve. When coolant comes out of the valve, retighten the bleed screw. Continue adding coolant to the bottle, to 3 cm (1 in.) above the 'maximum' mark. Refit the cap to the expansion bottle.

109F

making it easy! Old hoses become very set in their ways, and should you need to renew one you may find that, even with its clips fully slackened off, it will be reluctant to budge.
• Rather than employ too much force, particularly on a radiator, where there's a high risk of fracturing the hose stub, simply slide the clip out of the way and use a strong, sharp knife to slit the hose until you can open it up and peel it off the stub.
• Thoroughly clean the stubs, carefully using a file and emery cloth if necessary, to remove the lumpy corrosion often found on elderly alloy cooling system components.
• Position new clips (preferably) of flat, 'worm-drive' type) on the new hose, ensuring their tightening screws are best placed for easy screwdriver access when the hose is fitted. A smear of washing-up fluid will help the hose slide fully home on the stubs. Tighten the clips firmly, but don't bury them in the hose.

109G

SAFETY FIRST!
Never run the engine with the caps and the bleed screw open.

Warm up the engine (1) until the electric fan starts, then run for a further 5 minutes with bursts up to about 3000rpm to speed up the bleeding.

Stop the engine. Return the expansion bottle to its mounting. When the engine has cooled completely (after about 2 hours) check that the level is near the maximum and top up if necessary.

109H

LATER MODELS WITH FIXED EXPANSION TANK

109G. Add coolant and water directly to the expansion tank - DO NOT remove the radiator cap.

109H. Unscrew the bleed valve (arrowed) on the heater hose to release trapped air, closing it when coolant appears.

☐ **Job 110. Check/renew coolant expansion tank cap.**

INSIDE INFORMATION: The cooling system is under pressure when the engine is hot. This raises the boiling point of the coolant so that the engine can run at its most efficient temperature. If the expansion tank cap does not hold pressure, the coolant can boil and form steam pockets inside the engine with local overheating and damage.

110. Check the rubber sealing ring in the cap (arrowed) for signs of splitting or perishing, especially in the metal type of cap. Renew it if not in good condition.

110

☐ **Job 111. Renew drive belts.**

Replace the alternator and/or air-pump drive belts - see *Job 20* for details.

Every 36,000 Miles - or Every Three Years, whichever comes first

112A

112B

☐ **Job 112. Change gearbox oil/transmission fluid.**

Refer to pages 47 and 48 for details of topping up each of the various gearbox types.

> *SAFETY FIRST!*
> *As with engine oil, gearbox lubricants contain many chemicals that your hands may be sensitive to, so always wear rubber gloves when carrying out work that may bring oil into contact with the hands.*

'MA'-TYPE GEARBOX

112A. Position a container beneath and remove the drain plug from the gearbox; allow several minutes for the oil to drain completely. Some drain plugs are fitted with a magnet to collect any swarf (metal particles) that may be suspended in the oil - clean it off with a rag.

EARLY BE TYPE GEARBOXES (UP TO 1986)

112B. These are drained via the two drain plugs (2 and 3 in illustration). Oil is replenished through the combined filler/vent plug (1) located on top of the gearbox casing. (Illustration, courtesy Peugeot Talbot Motor Co Plc)

LATER 'BE'-TYPE GEARBOX

112C. This is the location of the single drain plug on these types - undo it with a spanner.

112D. Use a spanner to remove the filler/level plug on BE type gearboxes (FROM 1986), and fill through the hole. Access to the filler plug is gained easily through the passenger-side front wheelarch.

☐ **Job 113. Renew camshaft belt.**

INSIDE INFORMATION: The camshaft drive belt or 'cam-belt' performs the vital job of turning the camshaft in time with the crankshaft, from which it is driven. If it breaks, or the 'teeth' become stripped (the belt is made from rubber-reinforced fabric) then synchronisation will be lost and the camshaft-driven valves are likely to come into contact with the pistons, causing severe damage to the engine.

112C

112D

113. Special equipment is needed to check the tension of the cam belt - your Peugeot dealer will use this tension gauge to carry out the check quickly and accurately. (Illustration, courtesy Peugeot Talbot Motor Co Plc)

113

SPECIALIST SERVICE & INSIDE INFORMATION: Peugeot recommend that the cam-belt is changed at 36,000 miles or FOUR years for all petrol engined cars, with diesels at 72,000 miles or eight years. We would recommend playing safe and sticking to 36,000 miles or THREE years for all cars. A cam-belt breaks without warning and, as stated above, an engine can be very severely damaged as the pistons hit the valves. Replacement is a job is best entrusted to a reputable garage or Peugeot agent, who have the necessary facilities and skills to carry it out.

☐ **Job 114. Top up rustproofing.**

Apply rustproofing fluid/wax to the exposed areas of the car i.e. wheelarches and underside, where existing treatments are likely to be washed away by road grit and water. Apply 'proofer to the box sections and door interiors too, although it isn't necessary to use as much fluid as the original treatment. See *Chapter 5, Rustproofing*, for details.

Every 48,000 Miles - or Every Four Years, whichever comes first

☐ **Job 115. Renew HT leads, distributor cap and rotor arm.**

115. Even though the HT leads, distributor cap and rotor arm may look OK, they can deteriorate with age. To ensure trouble-free starting and running it pays to renew them at this interval.

making it easy! / *Mark the old cap with typists' correction fluid to indicate which lead goes to which plug; remove the old cap and leads from the distributor and use the markings as a guide to fitting the new leads.*

115

Every 72,000 Miles - or Every Six Years, whichever comes first

☐ **Job 116. Renew glow plugs.**

DIESEL ENGINES ONLY

Poor starting can be the bane of life for owners of older diesel engines. Replacing the glow plugs at this stage can make a major difference. See *Job 82* for details.

☐ **Job 117. Check and renew fuel injectors.**

FUEL INJECTION PETROL AND DIESEL ENGINES

117. In time, and even with detergent fuels, injectors become carboned and do not work at their full efficiency. This may show up as poor starting or a 'fail'-point on an MoT exhaust emission test. Checking the spray pattern of injectors calls for specialised equipment, so this is a job for **SPECIALIST SERVICE**. (Illustration courtesy of V.L.Churchill)

117

CHAPTER 4 - BODYWORK

In this Chapter, we show you how to make your car look its best. First, we demonstrate that your car's appearance can be improved beyond recognition by a couple of hours of work on a Sunday morning. Then, just in case a passing gate post should leap out at you, we explain how to carry out simple bodywork repairs at home.

PART I: THE BODY BEAUTIFUL

Have you ever looked in amazement at the condition of cars on a dealer's forecourt and wondered why your car doesn't look like that? Well, it can! It's all a matter of know-how and a bit of hard work - and using the techniques described in this Chapter, you'll find that your car can be made to look almost like new again, without using too many cans of elbow grease!

☐ I.1 Apply a thin coat of modern car polish, to give a far longer-lasting shine than old-fashioned waxes (though we've yet to find one that lasts as long as claimed!). Cover just one section of the car at a time and then, as soon as the wax dries to a haze, buff off for a superb shine. You'll see the dull paint and oxides come off on the cloth as you buff.

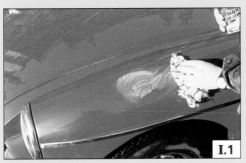

I.1

making it easy! • As you polish, keep turning the cloth, always presenting a clean face to the surface of the paint - that's the secret of obtaining a clear shine with no rub marks. You'll need several clean cloths for polishing a whole car!

• Try removing a bug splat with a kitchen abrasive pad - the gentler sort made for non-stick pans - but only on glass and chrome; it'll ruin the shine on paintwork.

☐ I.2 Weekend trips in your car are likely to be cursed by the 'bugs on the bumper' syndrome, as well as black tar on the bodywork. Soak all the bug-splatted areas with soapy water first, while you wash the rest of the car, then come back later, when they've been softened. Rub off with cloth, rather than a sponge. Use a proprietary brand of tar remover to wipe off tar splash.

SOFT-TOP SPORTS CARS: If your vinyl soft-top has ingrained dirt, scrub it gently all over with a nail brush and soapy water. When dry, apply a good quality vinyl cleaner to bring the appearance back like new. Fabric soft-tops should only be washed, not scrubbed, but can be hosed off to shift the dirt.

I.2

☐ I.3 It's easy to forget that around a fifth of your car's 'bodywork' is in fact glass. Use purpose-made glass cleaner, or a clean wash leather, for sparkling results. Clouding on the inside (said to be the vapour from upholstery plastics!) cleans off in the same way.

I.3

☐ I.4 Tyres are one of the most 'visual' parts of your car. There are proprietary tyre polishes and paints available, but be warned that the improvement in appearance goes the first time you drive on a wet road! A good cleaning with the wash sponge - *after* you've washed the rest of the car - is usually enough. Alloy wheels need a spray-on alloy wheel cleaner to shift stuck-on brake dust.

I.4

☐ *I.5 INSIDE INFORMATION: Many people just don't know what to do about dull plastic bumpers. Use a colourless trim cleaner and you'll find that just wiping it on will bring about a magical improvement. Several coats may be needed. (The old, black-coloured bumper polish makes a real mess of your hands, by the way!)*

☐ I.6 Even when an engine bay is clean, it often looks dirty. Use a spray-on cleaner to remove the heavy dirt and grease - best if you let it soak in to the worst areas. Use an old paintbrush in nooks and crannies. A vinyl protectant will then bring up a wonderful sheen to all of your hoses and pipes as well as all underbonnet paintwork.

I.5

making it easy! If your engine is very oily, ask a local garage with a steam cleaner to hose off the worst of the 'grunge' before starting to clean up the engine bay. Paint any bare metal exposed by the steam cleaning, before it starts to rust.

☐ I.7 Choose a vinyl cleaner designed to put back the suppleness into vinyl and protect it from fading, as well as to remove dirt and grime and restore the appearance. If you hate the 'tacky' high gloss shine produced by some of them, look out for the low-gloss variety, giving a more natural finish.

INSIDE INFORMATION: If you can't get hold of low-gloss vinyl cleaner, try wiping over with a damp cloth before the cleaner has fully dried. This also 'wipes' away the worst of the gloss.

Rubber seals will last far longer if they are protected against the elements, by regular treatments with vinyl and rubber protectant. Scrape out dirt and grit from around the lower door seals then treat them all with several coats.

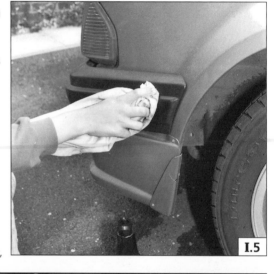

I.6

☐ I.8 Fabric seats and carpets will certainly benefit from cleaning with a proprietary brand of spray-on car upholstery cleaner - or a household upholstery cleaner. Follow the instructions carefully, take care not to soak cloth trim (it could cause shrinking) and the result will be carpets and cloth seats that look like new.

You can make leather more supple, and keep it cleaner and longer lasting by using a purpose-made brand of leather care. After use, the leather will feel soft and supple, because of the lanolin and moisturisers that you will have added. At first, you may be surprised to see the colour of your leather go much darker but don't worry; that will pass as the leather cleaner dries out naturally.

I.7

I.8

PART II: REPAIRING BODYWORK BLEMISHES

However well you look after your car, there will always be the risk of car park accident damage - or even worse! The smallest paint chips are best touched up with paint purchased from your local auto. accessory shop. If your colour of paint is not available, some auto. accessory shops offer a mixing scheme (including aerosols, in some cases) or you could look for a local paint factor in Yellow Pages. Take your car along to the paint factor and have them match the colour and mix the smallest quantity of cellulose paint that they will supply you with. Larger body blemishes will need the use of body filler.

SAFETY FIRST!
***Always** wear plastic gloves when working with body filler, before it has set. Always wear a face mask when sanding filler and wear goggles when using a power sander.*

☐ II.1 The rear of this car's bodywork has sustained a nasty gash, the sort of damage for which you will certainly need to use body filler. The first stage is to mask off. Try to find "natural" edges such as body mouldings or styling stripes and wherever you can, mask off body trim rather than having to remove it.

☐ II.2 Remove all paint from the damaged area and for about 25mm (1 in.) around the damaged area. Roughen the bare metal or surface with coarse abrasive paper - a power sander is best. Wipe over the area with white spirit (mineral spirit) and then wash off with washing-up liquid in water - *not* car wash detergent.

INSIDE INFORMATION: Rub the surrounding paintwork with cutting compound so that the new paint has a better chance of matching the old.

☐ II.3 Mix the filler and hardener, following the instructions on the can. It's best to use a piece of plastic or metal rather than cardboard because otherwise, the filler will pick up fibres from the surface of the card. Mix thoroughly until the colour is consistent and no traces of hardener can be discerned.

☐ II.4 You can now spread the filler evenly over the repair. If the damage is particularly deep, apply the paste in two or more layers, allowing the filler to harden before adding the next layer. The final layer should be just proud of the level required, but do not overfill as this wastes paste and will require more time to sand down.

☐ II.5 It is essential when sanding down that you wrap the sanding paper around a flat block. You can see from the scratch marks that this repair has been sanded diagonally in alternate directions until the filler has become level with the surrounding panel, but you have to take care not to go deeply into the edges of the paint around the repair.

INSIDE INFORMATION: There will invariably be small pin holes even if the right amount of filler was applied first time. Use a tiny amount of filler scraped very thin over the whole repair, filling in deep scratches and pin holes and then sanding off with a very fine grade of sand paper - preferably dry paper rather than wet-or-dry because you don't want to get water on to the bare filler.

BODYWORK

☐ II.6 You can now use an aerosol primer to spray over the whole area of the repair but preferably not right up to the edges of the masking tape...

☐ II.7 ...and now use wet-or-dry paper, again on a sanding block, to sand the primer paint.

INSIDE INFORMATION: Don't sand fresh primer paint - leave it up to a day to harden off.

The filler is now protected from the water by the paint. If you do apply paint right up to the edge of the tape, be sure to 'feather' the edges of the primer, so that the edges blend in smoothly to the surrounding surface, with no ridges.

SAFETY FIRST!
Always wear an efficient mask when spraying aerosol paint and only work in a well-ventilated area, well away from any source of ignition, because spray paint vapour, even that given off by an aerosol, is highly flammable. Ensure that you have doors and windows open to the outside when using aerosol paint but in cool or damp weather, close them when the vapour has dispersed, otherwise the surface of the paint will "bloom", or take on a milky appearance. In fact, you may find it difficult to obtain a satisfactory finish in cold or damp weather.

☐ II.8 Before starting to spray, ensure that the nozzle is clear. Note that the can must be held with the index finger well back on the aerosol button. If you let your finger overhang the front of the button, a paint drip can form and throw itself on to the work area as a paint blob.

making it easy! • One of the secrets of spraying paint which doesn't run, is to put a very light coat of spray paint on to the panel first, followed by several more coats, allowing time between each coat for the bulk of the solvent to evaporate.

• Alternate coats should go on horizontally, followed by vertical coats as shown on the inset diagram.

☐ II.9 After allowing about a week for the paint to dry, you will be able to polish it with a light cutting compound, blending the edges of the repair into the surrounding paintwork.

*INSIDE INFORMATION: Do note that if your repairs don't work out first time and you have to apply more paint on top of the fresh paint that you have already used, allow a week to elapse otherwise there is a strong risk of pickling or other reactions to take place. Also note that a prime cause of paint failure is the existence of silicones on the surface of the old paint before you start work. These come from most types of polish and are not all that easy to remove - they **won't** sand off!. Thoroughly wipe the panel down with white spirit before starting work and wash off with warm water and washing-up liquid to remove any further traces of the polish and the white spirit - but don't use the sponge or bucket that you normally use for washing the car otherwise you will simply introduce more silicones onto the surface!*

CHAPTER 5 - RUSTPROOFING

When mechanical components deteriorate, they can cost you a lot of money to replace. But when your car's bodywork deteriorates, it can cost you the car, if corrosion goes beyond the point where repairs are economical to carry out. Rust prevention should be regarded as a regular maintenance job, one which enables you to extend the life of your car by many years - and that will save you *real* money!

If you want to prolong its life, you'll have to inject rustproofing fluid into all the enclosed box sections and 'chassis' sections on your car. In many cases, you'll find holes already in place; in others, you'll be able to take off a cover, a piece or trim or a door lock in order to gain access. But in quite a few cases, you'll need to drill holes to gain an entry.

making it easy! Decide on your drill size with reference to the size of the injector nozzle and the size of grommets that you can obtain for blanking the holes off again afterwards. You'll feel a bit foolish if you drill first, only to find that they don't make grommets to fit the holes you've drilled!

Choose Your Weapon

Those hand pump injectors that you can buy from DIY shops are often worse than useless. They don't usually make a proper spray, but simply squirt a jet of fluid that does nothing to give the all-over cover required. Make a dummy 'box section' out of a cardboard box - cut it and fold to make it about 10 or 15 cm square - and try a dummy run. Open up and see if it has worked. If you haven't obtained full misting of the fluid, you could be making the problem worse.

INSIDE INFORMATION: Rust strikes even harder in those areas that aren't properly covered!

Consider taking your car to a garage with suitable equipment and having them do the work for you. Full, professional injection equipment, as shown in the following picture sequence, will make the fluid reach much further and deeper than amateur equipment, and if you enlist the services of the best experts as featured here, you'll be able to benefit from their experience.

Don't be a drip!

Place *lots* of newspaper beneath the car to catch the inevitable drips. Some seat belts retract into a cavity that you will want to spray with fluid. Pull each belt out and hold it there until you have finished spraying the fluid. All electric motors should be covered up with plastic bags so that none of the rustproofing fluid gets in and all windows should be fully wound up. Ensure that all drain channels are clear so that any excess rustproofing fluid can drain out and also check once again that they are clear after you have finished carrying out the work to ensure that your application of the fluid has not caused them to be clogged up, otherwise water will become trapped, negating much of the good work you have carried out.

SAFETY FIRST!
Before using rustproofer, read the manufacturer's safety notes. Keep rustproofing fluid off the exhaust or any other components where it could be ignited. Keep it away from brake components, covering them up with plastic bags before starting work. Follow Chapter 1, Safety First!, and advice at the start of Chapter 3, Servicing Your Car especially with regard to safe working beneath a car raised off the ground. Rustproofers all contain solvents. In a confined space, such as a garage, solvents can build up, creating both a health and a fire hazard. Wear an efficient face mask so that you don't inhale vapour and work out of doors, keeping out of confined spaces. Wear gloves and goggles, but if you do get any fluid in your eyes, wash out with copious amounts of water and immediately seek medical advice if necessary. If any welding has to be carried out on the vehicle within a few months of rust-proofing being carried out, you must inform those who are carrying out the work because of the fire risk.

Our thanks are due to Castles Ltd, Leicester, for help in preparing this chapter and for making a car available for photography and to Dinol Ltd for supplying their Dinitrol rustproofing fluid.

RUSTPROOFING

☐ Job 1. Clean underbody

You will have to hose off the underside of the body, paying particular attention to the undersides of the wings and wheel arches, before you can start to apply new rustproofing. Scrape off any hard, thick deposits of mud, and any old flaking body sealant under the car.

1. One of the quickest ways to do the job is to use a power washer with a long lance. Many garages have this equipment for customer use in a wash bay and this is a very efficient way of doing the job. You will, however, still have to go underneath with a scraper afterwards as even a power jet won't take off flaking body sealant. You will also have to wait up to a week for the underside of the car to dry thoroughly (in warm, dry weather) before applying new rustproofing.

☐ Job 2. Equipment.

Gather together all the materials you need to do the job before you start. There are a number of products available for d.i.y. use, some of which are shown. You will also need lifting equipment and axle stands.

> *making it easy!* 2. A compressor-driven gun of this type won't break the bank - try your local motor trade parts factors - but you'll need to buy or hire a compressor. Results will be perfect.

Bear in mind the safety equipment you will need - referred to in *Safety First! - see page 81.* You will need copious amounts of newspaper to spread on the floor because quite a lot of rustproofing fluid will run out of the box sections and other areas under the car and you may have to park your car over newspaper for a couple of days after carrying out this treatment. Remember that the vapour given off by the materials will continue for several days, so park your car in the open for a week or so if you can, rather than in an enclosed garage.

Around the Car

☐ Job 3. Chrome trim and seams

3. Some rustproofing fluids in aerosol cans are thin enough for injecting behind chromium trim strips and badges but some people find that they are inclined to leave a stain on the paintwork around the trim. As an alternative to a rustproofing fluid, you can use a water dispersant or a thin oil.

☐ Job 4. Doors.

4A. Remove the trim panel and carefully 'peel' away the clear plastic membrane that covers the door inner cavity. Insert the nozzle to cover all the inside of the door, making sure you get plenty of 'creeping' fluid into the steel joints, where water could collect and corrosion could occur.

4B

5

4B. A common problem is that moisture collects in the bottom of the doors and rots them out from the inside, so use plenty of fluid here. If you don't want to remove the door trims, then fluid can be sprayed through the lower drain slots, but note that this will only provide protection for the lower surfaces and seams. Also, make sure that any audio speakers fitted to the door are temporarily removed while spraying takes place.

☐ Job 5. The 'A' post.

5. The 'A' post box-section is that part of the body immediately behind the front wings to which the front doors are hinged. Access is gained by unscrewing the courtesy light switch (via a single securing screw) and inserting a flexible nozzle as far as it will go, spraying as it is withdrawn. Feed the nozzle in both directions (up and down) so that all inner surfaces are covered, paying particular attention to the bottom of the section.

☐ Job 6. The 'B' post.

6A. 205s have a grommet fitted to the lower 'B' post (the box section that connects the roof to the floor and onto which the doors close) which gives adequate access if a flexible nozzle is inserted and worked up into the post....

6B. ... and down to its joint with the sill.

INSIDE INFORMATION: Think carefully before drilling holes to insert rustproofing fluid, especially in the 'chassis', where there are numerous holes already. If you do drill a hole in steel, make sure that you file off the rough burrs and then apply an anti-rusting agent, followed by a coating of paint followed by a layer of wax. Make sure the area you drill into is indeed hollow and not the inside of the car or luggage bay! Spend time looking out for wires or pipes. Disconnect the car's battery.

☐ Job 7. The 'C' post.

7. Treat the lower section of the 'C' post (just ahead of the rear wheel arches) through this grommet', passing the flexible nozzle through as far as it will go in each direction, spraying as it is withdrawn. Pay particular attention to the upper surfaces which are a vulnerable rot-spot' on all cars - make sure this area is adequately treated with fluid.

6A

6B

7

☐ Job 8. Tailgate.

8. These drain holes provide good access to the tailgate interior, although it is best if the trim can be removed. Direct the flexible nozzle into all the strengthening ribs and seams, spraying as the nozzle is drawn out. 'Wiggle' the nozzle up into the sides of the tailgate around the rear screen aperture if possible, otherwise apply copious rustproofer and allow it to 'run' down the channels. When spraying is complete, close the tailgate so that fluid drains down into the bottom seam. Make sure the drain holes remain clear on the bottom edge.

☐ Job 9. Boot/luggage bay area.

9. Remove the pull-away side trims and work the nozzle into the space between the outer wing and the boot/luggage bay 'floor', paying particular attention to the lower joint which forms the wheel arch. It is a good idea to remove the rear lights also, in order to reach the box section beneath them and to adequately treat the upper corners of the wing. Insert the flexible nozzle into the box section that crosses the boot at the rear - holes provided for the wiring harness will give access to this section. Spray the spare wheel compartment (after removing the wheel!) but remember to wipe the excess fluid away before replacing it.

☐ Job 10. Bonnet.

10. Inject fluid into all strengthening ribs and channels on the underside of the bonnet. Some models have a fibre-board insulation cover clipped to the underside - remove this first. Pay attention to the front, rear, and side-seams of the bonnet, making sure sufficient fluid is applied to penetrate the layers of metal. As with the tailgate, close the bonnet after application so that fluid runs down to the front seam.

☐ Job 11. Engine bay.

11A. Remember to treat the joints between wings and body and to the wing fixing bolts/washers. Apply fluid behind and beneath the front 'slam' panel, down the seams between inner wing and bulkhead, and around the headlight/sidelight apertures.

11B. Rustproof the inner corners of the 'apron' at the rear of the engine bay, reaching the seam beneath the panel where the windscreen is fixed, and around the wiper motor and heater blower box. At each end of the rear apron, work the nozzle up into the windscreen pillars, spraying as it is withdrawn.

8

9

10

11A

11B

11C

11C. Apply fluid to the suspension tops, around the projecting studs and nuts, and also to the edges of the over-lapping panels on the suspension turrets.

Under the Car

☐ **Job 12. Cross members.**

12A. Work the flexible nozzle along the cross-member and spray as it is withdrawn, paying particular attention to the end-seams where they join the inner wing 'out-riggers' that travel forwards through the engine bay; use the flexible nozzle to treat these sections too, gaining access through the many drain holes already provided.

12A

12B. The centre and rear cross-members are similarly treated - all these sections contain suitable apertures for the nozzle to enter.

12C. Treat the longitudinal body sections, like this one which supports the front floors.

☐ **Job 13. Sills.**

Work the flexible nozzle into each hole, in both fore and aft directions, each time spraying as it is withdrawn. Small drainage holes are present on the sill panels - make sure these are clear by poking with a short length of stiff wire. Fluid should issue from all such holes, if you've applied it sufficiently!

12B

making it easy! 13A. The sills are provided with rubber drain plugs at manufacture, so it is not necessary to drill holes to ensure coverage.

12C

13A

13B. Treat this area at the inner rear sill panel where it joins the rear wheel arch, using the hole provided. Apply fluid in all directions and insert the probe as far as it will go.

☐ Job 14. Front and rear 'chassis' sections.

14. Treat those chassis areas at front and rear that travel across the car - that shown is the join between the front chassis side-rail (or outrigger) and the front apron/radiator surround.

☐ Job 15. Spray underside and wheel arches.

Get yourself prepared for this job! Disposable overalls or old clothes are a necessity and none more so than some form of headgear to protect your hair. Gloves and a face-mask are also essential.

13B

15. First of all, the thinner, 'creeping' type of fluid is sprayed into and onto every seam. (This goes quite a long way into every joint but would wash away if not covered over.) Then, it's time to cover the entire surface with the tougher type of protectant. For this process the thicker, black underbody fluid is used - note that this needs to be warmed by standing it in a bucket of very hot water for twenty minutes or so before use. Make doubly sure that the car is safely raised and stable - this is no time to take chances - and ensure any floor protection is in place and secure.

Spray the fluid while it is still warm and 'thin' taking care to ensure an even coverage with no gaps. When spraying over fuel and brake pipes make at least two passes with the spray gun, at different angles, so that the fluid isn't masked by the pipes which would leave an unprotected 'shadow' behind them. Start at the front of the car and work backwards, ending with the boot underside and spare wheel well.

14

☐ Job 16. The wheel arches.

16. Remove all four wheels and wrap plastic bags around the brake discs or drums. If your car is fitted with plastic 'inner splashguards' it's a good idea to remove them so that the fluid can be applied to the 'hidden' seams and surfaces, because they can still get damp, if not wet, and consequently will corrode. Pay particular attention to the outer wheel arch seams - spray 'outwards' from inside the wheelarch to ensure good penetration and sealing. Spray also up into the coil spring recesses (suspension tops), varying the angle of the spray gun as the fluid is applied.

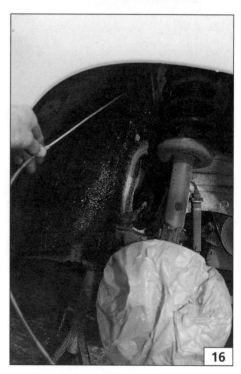

16

making it easy! Tip from Dinol, the manufacturers of Dinitrol: Except in a heat wave, it is essential to stand the container of rustproofer in a tub of hot water to keep it fluid. Top up the tub from time to time with more hot water while you are working. Not only will warm rustproofer penetrate seams better, it will flow through the applicator better and not clog so easily. Some people thin the rustproofer with white spirit, but warming it is better. Wash the gun and lances out with white spirit afterwards. If you let the rustproofer set, it is almost impossible to clean them.

Finally, clean any fluid 'overspray' from the body work, including the door sills where fluid will have dripped from the door drain holes. Use a good glass cleaner if fluid has found its way onto the windows (it usually does!), especially the windscreen. Also, clean the windscreen wiper blades, as traces of fluid will be smeared across the screen when the wipers are next used and you're unlikely to see much through it! The last job is to fit any grommets into holes you may have drilled - soak them in fluid before fitting, which will provide a very effective seal when the fluid turns to wax over the next week or so.

CHAPTER 6 - FAULT FINDING

Does this sound familiar? The vehicle refuses to start one damp Sunday morning. You decide that there must be no fuel getting through. By the time you've stripped the fuel pump and fuel lines and "unblocked" the fuel tank, it's time for bed. And the next day, the local garage finds that your main HT lead has dropped out of the coil! Something like that has happened to most of us!

Don't jump to conclusions: if your engine won't start or runs badly, if electrical components fail, follow the logical sequence of checks listed here and detailed overleaf, eliminating each "check" (by testing, not by "hunch") before moving on to the next. And remember that the great majority of failures are caused by electrical or ignition faults: only a minor proportion of engine failures come from the fuel system. Follow the sequences shown here - and you'll have a better chance of success in finding that fault. Before carrying out any of the work described in this Chapter please read carefully *Chapter 1, Safety First!*

PART I - PETROL ENGINED VEHICLES

Engine won't start.

1. Starter motor doesn't turn.

2. Is battery okay?

3. Check battery connections for cleanliness/ tightness.

4. Have battery 'drop' test carried out by specialist.

5. Test battery with voltmeter or, preferable, with a hydrometer.

6. Can engine be rotated by hand?

7. If engine cannot be rotated by hand, check for mechanical seizure of power unit, or pinion gear jammed in mesh with flywheel - 'rock' car backwards and forwards until free, or apply spanner to square drive at front end of starter motor.

8. If engine can be rotated by hand, check for loose electrical connections at starter, faulty solenoid, or defective starter motor.

9. Starter motor turns slowly.

10. Battery low on charge or defective - re-charge and have 'drop' test carried out by specialist.

11. Internal fault within starter motor - e.g. worn brushes.

12. Starter motor noisy or harsh.

13. Drive teeth on ring gear or starter pinion worn/broken.

14. Main drive spring broken.

15. Starter motor securing bolts loose.

16. Starter motor turns engine but car will not start. See 'Ignition System' box.

Ignition system.

> **SAFETY FIRST!**
> *It is essential that you read **Chapter 1, Safety First!, The Ignition System** before carrying out work on this part of the car.*

(Carry out the following checks as appropriate. For example, some vehicles have contact breaker ignition while the majority of modern cars have electronic ignition. Only Step 17 can be carried out on cars with electronic ignition. If any faults are found - **SPECIALIST SERVICE**.)

17. Check for spark at plug (remove plug and prop it with threads resting on bare metal of cylinder block). Do not touch plug or lead while operating starter.

MODELS WITHOUT ELECTRONIC IGNITION ONLY

18. If no spark present at plug, check for spark at contact breaker points when 'flicked' open (ignition 'on'). Double-check to ensure that points are clean and correctly gapped, and try again.

19. If spark present at contact breaker points, check for spark at central high tension lead from coil. NOTE: Don't carry out this check with electronic ignition systems. An uncontrolled spark can, in some cases, seriously damage the ECU (Electronic Control Unit).

20. If spark present at central high tension lead from coil, check distributor cap and rotor arm; replace if cracked or contacts badly worn.

21. If distributor cap and rotor arm are okay, check high tension leads and connections - replace leads if they are old, carbon core type suppressed variety.

22. If high tension leads are sound but dirty or damp, clean/dry them.

23. If high tension leads okay, check/clean/dry/re-gap sparking plugs.

24. Damp conditions? Apply water dispellant spray to ignition system.

25. If no spark present at contact breaker points (cars without electronic ignition only), examine connections of low tension leads between ignition switch and coil, and from coil to contact breaker (including short low-tension lead within distributor).

26. If low tension circuit connections okay, examine wiring.

27. If low tension wiring is sound, is capacitor okay? If in doubt, fit new capacitor.

28. If capacitor is okay, check for spark at central high tension lead from coil. NOTE: DON'T carry out this check with electronic ignition systems. An uncontrolled spark can, in some cases, seriously damage the ECU (Electronic Control Unit).

29. If no spark present at central high tension lead from coil, check for poor high tension lead connections.

30. If high tension lead connections okay, is coil okay? If in doubt, fit new coil.

31. If spark present at plug, is it powerful or weak? If weak, see '27' (non-electronic ignition models only).

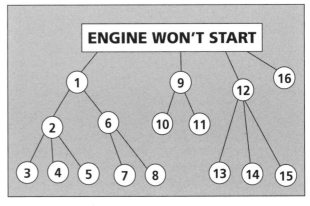

FAULT FINDING

32. If spark is healthy, check ignition timing.

33. If ignition timing is okay, see 'Fuel System' box.

Fuel system.

FUEL INJECTED ENGINES ONLY

34. Do not disconnect fuel pipes to check fuel flow, as system is pressurised; check fuel pump operation by listening for "buzz" when ignition is switched on - buzz should last no more than 1 or 2 seconds; if longer, suspect fuel pump. If no buzz, suspect fuel pump relay - seek professional help.

NON FUEL INJECTED ENGINES ONLY

35. Check briefly for fuel at feed pipe to carb. See 36. If no fuel present at feed pipe, is petrol tank empty? (Rock car and listen for 'sloshing' in tank, as well as looking at gauge).

36. Check for a defective fuel pump. With outlet pipe disconnected AND AIMED AWAY FROM HOT EXHAUST COMPONENTS, ETC. as well as your eyes and clothes, and into a suitable container, turn the engine over (manual pump) or switch on ignition (electric pump) and fuel should issue from pump outlet.

37. If pump is okay, check for blocked fuel filter or pipe, or major leak in pipe between tank and pump, or between pump and carb.

38. If the filter is clean and the pump operates, suspect blocked carburettor jet(s) or damaged/ sticking float, or incorrectly adjusted carburettor.

39. If there is petrol in the tank but none issues from the feed pipe from pump to carburettor, check that the small vent hole in the fuel filler cap is not blocked and causing a vacuum. NOTE: On some cars there is no vent hole in the filler cap. Other arrangements are made for venting the tank. There are many systems - **SPECIALIST SERVICE**.

40. If fuel is present at carburettor feed pipe, remove spark plugs and check whether wet with unburnt fuel.

41. If the spark plugs are fuel-soaked, check that the choke is operating as it should and is not jammed 'shut'. Other possibilities include float needle valve(s) sticking 'open' or leaking, float punctured, carburettor incorrectly adjusted or air filter totally blocked. Clean plugs before replacing.

42. If the spark plugs are dry, check whether the float needle valve is jammed 'shut'.

43. Check for severe air leak at inlet manifold gasket or carburettor gasket. Incorrectly set valve clearances.

Engine lacks power.

44. Engine overheating. Check oil temperature gauge (where fitted). Low oil pressure light may come on.

45. Air cleaner intake thermostat not opening/closing at the correct temperatures. Replace or free-off as necessary.

46. If thermostat okay, check oil level. BEWARE - DIPSTICK AND OIL MAY BE VERY HOT.

47. If oil level okay, check for slipping fan belt, cylinder head gasket 'blown', partial mechanical seizure of engine, blocked or damaged exhaust system.

48. If engine temperature is normal, check cylinder compressions.

49. If cylinder compression readings low, add a couple of teaspoons of engine oil to each cylinder in turn, and repeat test. If readings don't improve, suspect burnt valves/seats.

50. If compression readings improve after adding oil as described, suspect worn cylinder bores, pistons and rings.

51. If compression readings are normal, check for mechanical problems, for example, binding brakes, slipping clutch, partially seized transmission, etc.

Engine stops suddenly.

52. Check for sudden ingress of water/snow onto ignition components, in adverse weather conditions. Sudden failure is almost always because of an ignition fault. Check for simple wiring and connection breakdowns.

Lights fail.

53. Sudden failure - check fuses.

54. If all lamps affected, check switch and main wiring feeds.

55. If not all lamps are affected, check bulbs on lamps concerned.

56. If bulbs appear to be okay, check bulb holder(s), local wiring and connections.

57. If bulb(s) blown, replace!

58. Intermittent operation, flickering or poor light output.

59. Check earth (ground) connections(s).

60. If earth(s) okay, check switch.

61. If switch okay, check wiring and connections.

Horn failure.

62. If horn does not operate, check fuse, all connections (particularly earths/grounds) and cables. Remove horn connections and check/clean. Use 12v test lamp to ascertain power getting to horn.

63. If horn will not stop(!), disconnect the horn and check for earthing of cable between button and horn unit and the wiring and contacts in the

horn switch housing. **SPECIALIST SERVICE.** Horn wiring and connections are more complex than they appear at first. If necessary, have them checked by a specialist.

Fuel gauge problems.

64. Gauge reads 'empty' - check for fuel in tank!

65. If fuel is present in tank, check for earthing of wiring from tank to gauge, and for wiring disconnections.

66. Gauge permanently reads 'full', regardless of tank contents. Check wiring and connections as in '65'.

67. If wiring and connections all okay, sender unit/fuel gauge defective.

68. With wiring disconnected, check for continuity between fuel gauge terminals. Do NOT test gauge by short-circuiting to earth. Replace unit if faulty.

69. If gauge is okay, disconnect wiring from tank sender unit and check for continuity between terminal and case. Replace sender unit if faulty.

PART II - DIESEL ENGINE FAULT FINDING

SAFETY FIRST! Working on a diesel engine is no more dangerous than any other but remember that, when cranking the engine on the starter or even turning it over by hand, it could start. In theory the fuel cut-off valve should prevent this, but don't rely upon it.

Diesel fuel can cause skin disorders, so it's *essential* to use some form of barrier cream on your hands before starting work or to wear gloves. NEVER suck on a pipe in an attempt to draw up fuel.

INSIDE INFORMATION: When working on the fuel system, cleanliness is essential. Always wipe all unions clean before disconnecting, or even slackening them. The slightest trace of dust, water or any other contaminant can ruin the mirror-like finish on the 'internals' of the pump and injector plungers.

Engine won't start.

1. Starter Motor and Battery. Starter motor problems will be more or less the same as for petrol engines. However low cranking speeds

can prevent the engine from starting - see Check 11, Engine Condition.

2. Low pressure fuel system. The low pressure side of a diesel engined car fuel system is much the same as that in petrol versions comprising tank, filter and pump with interconnecting pipes. As such, you must check for the same kind of problems - air leaks into the system, fuel leaks from it and, of course, blockages.

3. No fuel in tank. If you run out of fuel, you will have to vent the system of air. The procedure for this can vary from model to model, but see the relevant section of *Chapter 3, Servicing Your Car.*

4. Fuel blockage. Usually if a lack of fuel is suspected, the first check will be at the bleed valve on the injection pump. Slacken this off and either operate the priming pump or crank the engine. No fuel coming out would indicate either an air leak or blockage, so repeat the test at the filter inlet. Any problems at this point would indicate a fault either at the tank itself, or between the tank and filter and would be much the same as those associated with a normal petrol system.

5. Fuel pump stop control. Check that the stop control solenoid at the pump clicks when the 'ignition' key is turned: If so you can assume it is working. If not, check for a 12 volt supply at the solenoid terminal ('ignition' on).

Other than actually running out of fuel, this is the most probable reason for lack of fuel at the injectors. A defective valve may also result in the engine continuing to run when switched off.

6. High pressure fuel system. *Safety First!* Beware very

high residual pressure in pipe when disconnecting even if engine not running! Pressure high enough for jet of diesel to penetrate skin - could cause blindness if it strikes the eye!

This part of the diesel engine's fuel system extends from the injection pump to the injectors. The pressures within the system are extremely high during the injection process (in the region of 300 bar) so care should be taken not to release any connections when the engine is running or being cranked on the starter motor. Checks on this part of the system are **SPECIALIST SERVICE** jobs other than the jobs shown below.

7. Injector pump faulty.

IMPORTANT NOTE: Testing the operation and output from the fuel injection pump requires specialist equipment. Do not attempt to strip it down yourself. Don't even remove it unless you are sure how to refit it and time it.

Some pumps are driven by a toothed belt, often the same one that drives the camshaft. As such they can suffer the same problems as with petrol engined cars - incorrect adjustment, overriding the teeth or complete breakage. Inspect the belt - if any problems, DON'T RUN THE ENGINE until you've had the belt replaced and the pump timed by a specialist.

8. Injectors faulty. As with the injection pump, specialised equipment is needed for checking the injectors. In some cases you can actually feel a light pulse on the injector feed pipe when injection takes place and the injector may also give a discernible grunt or buzz. However, neither is any indicator of a satisfactory injector spray pattern.

9. Injector feed pipes leaking. This would normally be pretty obvious with escaping fuel

leaving its mark. If only one injector is affected, the engine would probably start, but misfire and possibly emit black smoke. If the cause is a leaking union, then simply tightening it may sort out the problem. However, should the pipe itself be defective (cracked or split), the only answer is to renew it.

10. Glow plugs inoperative (cold engine). Glow plugs seldom go wrong, although after a considerable mileage, the heating elements may burn out. This would be unlikely to happen to all of the plugs at the same time, and if only one were affected, the engine would probably start but misfire on that cylinder until warmed up. Any failure affecting all of the plugs would probably be in the power supply. Symptoms of failure: engine slow to start; black smoke; misfiring until engine warm. Solution: replace any individual faulty plugs; check wiring if all are affected.

11. Engine condition. Combustion is achieved in diesel engines through heat generated by compressing air and anything which affects compression pressure - such as worn bores or 'leaking' valves - can result in poor starting or non-starting - much more so than with a petrol engine. Low cranking speeds may not have much effect on compression as such, but the consequent additional heat loss through the cylinder walls (due to the low piston speed) could also result in poor starting.

IMPORTANT NOTE: Do not use a petrol engine compression tester on a diesel engine - even assuming it could be held in place, because the high pressures involved would ruin it. Any such check should be left to the professionals. The same applies to checking valve clearances where any error could result in a valve striking the piston with consequent engine damage.

Engine misfires.

12. Water in fuel.

INSIDE INFORMATION: The adverse effects of water in fuel are more pronounced in a diesel engined car than the petrol equivalent and, depending upon severity, may result in a misfire or the engine failing to start. Water may also damage the injection equipment. Many diesel cars have a water trap built into the main fuel filter which should be drained at regular intervals. See **Chapter 3, Servicing Your Car**.

Unfortunately, if there is water in the system, it will all have to be drained of fuel - fuel tank, filter, fuel lines - and fresh fuel used. Dispose of scrap fuel responsibly at your nearest Local Authority disposal point.

13. Injection pump, injectors and engine condition. Most of the factors resulting in non-starting could also cause a misfire. See Checks 7, 8, 9 and 11.

Excessive smoke from exhaust.

14. Blue smoke. Results from oil being burnt in the combustion chamber. Causes similar to those for petrol engines - poor bore sealing,

worn valve guides or faulty valve stem seals. NB Brake fluid leaking into the engine via a faulty brake servo will also produce blue smoke, but you will notice a slow, steady loss of brake fluid if this is the problem. SPECIALIST SERVICE: HAVE THE PROBLEM ATTENDED TO WITHOUT DELAY!

15. White smoke (steam). White smoke is usually steam and 'disappears' into the air. Usually caused by water (coolant) leaking into engine or exhaust although a cold engine on a cold or damp day will emit steam, and this is acceptable. Causes can be similar to those for petrol engines - cracked block, cracked cylinder head, defective head gasket.

16. Black smoke. Injection pump faults such as excessive fuel delivery, low fuel pressures and incorrect timing could all result in black smoke from the exhaust. Poor spray patterns, dribble and other injector faults are also possible causes, all of which will require professional assistance.

FACT FILE: EMERGENCY STARTING

Pushing or Towing

NOTE: This is not possible for vehicles with automatic transmission. Diesel engines: only attempt in warm weather or with a warm engine.

Turn off all unnecessary electrical load; switch on ignition and depress the clutch pedal. Select second or third gear; release the clutch when the car reaches a person's running speed.

Starting with Jump Leads

Safety First!
This process can be dangerous and the following instructions must be followed to the letter. Also see **Chapter One, Safety First!** *and the relevant part of* **Chapter 3** *for information on safe handling of car batteries.*

Ensure that the battery providing the jump start has the same voltage (12 volt) as the battery fitted to your car.

Do not lean over the battery during jump starting.

Switch off all unnecessary electrical loads and apply the hand brake. Auto. Transmission: Place gear selector in 'P'. Manual Transmission: Place gear shift lever in neutral.

Note that on some batteries and on battery connections, '+' (positive) terminals are coloured red and '-' (negative) terminals are coloured blue or black.

Run the engine of the vehicle providing the jump start (if battery fitted to vehicle).

(The following instruction numbers refer to the numbers on the drawing.)

1. Connect one end of the jump lead to the positive ('+') terminal of the battery providing the jump start.

2. Connect the other end of the same lead to the positive terminal on the car being started.

3. Connect one end of the other jump lead to the negative ('-') terminal on the 'slave' battery...

4. ...and the other end to the negative battery lead on the car, or to some bare metal in the car's engine bay.

Now try to start the car as quickly as is reasonably possible.

IT IS IMPORTANT that the leads are removed in the exact reverse sequence to that shown above. Keep hands, hair and loose clothing away from moving parts in both engine bays.

CHAPTER 7
GETTING THROUGH THE MOT

This Chapter is for owners in Britain whose vehicles need to pass the 'MoT' test. The Test was first established in 1961 by the then Ministry of Transport and it attempts to ensure that vehicles using British roads reach minimum standards of safety. Approximately 40 per cent of vehicles submitted for the test fail it, but many of these failures could be avoided by knowing what the vehicle might 'fall down on', and by taking appropriate remedial action before the test 'proper' is carried out.

It is true that the scope of the test has been considerably enlarged in the past few years, with the result that it is correspondingly more difficult to be sure that your vehicle will reach the required standards. In truth, however, a careful examination of the relevant areas, perhaps a month or so before the current certificate expires, will highlight components which require attention, and enable any obvious faults to be rectified before you take the vehicle for the test.

On the other hand, a clean vehicle makes a better impression and it will help the examiner to see what he is supposed to be examining. Generally, this will work in the owner's favour. For example, if a component or an area of underbody or chassis is particularly difficult to examine due to a build-up of oily dirt etc., and if the examiner is in doubt about its condition, he is entitled to fail that component because it was not possible for him to conclude that it reached the required standard. Had it been clean, it might well have been tested, and passed!

MoT testers do not dismantle assemblies during the test but you may wish to do so during your pretest check-up for a better view of certain wearing parts, such as the rear brake

Getting Ahead

It is also worth noting that a vehicle can be submitted for a test up to a month before the current certificate expires - if the vehicle passes, the new certificate will be valid for one year from the day of expiry of the old one, provided that the old certificate is produced at the time of the test.

PART I: THE BACKGROUND

Keeping Up To Date

Alterations are being made to the Test on a regular basis - almost always making it tougher than it was before. It is MOST IMPORTANT that UK owners find out for themselves about any changes in the requirements that might have been made since this book was written. Your local MoT Testing Station should be able to help - if not, take your custom elsewhere! Also, non-UK owners should obtain information on the legal requirements in their own territory - and act accordingly.

Making A Good Impression

If your vehicle is muddy or particularly dirty (especially underneath) it would be worth giving it a thorough clean a day or two before carrying out the inspection so that it has ample time to dry. Do the same before the real MoT test. A clean vehicle makes a better impression on the examiner, who can refuse to test a vehicle which is particularly dirty underneath.

SAFETY FIRST!
The MoT tester will follow a set procedure and we will cover the ground in a similar way, starting inside the vehicle, then continuing outside, under the bonnet, underneath the vehicle, etc. When preparing to go underneath the vehicle, do ensure that it is jacked on firm level ground and then supported on axle stands or ramps which are adequate for the task. Wheels which remain on the ground should have chocks in front of and behind them, and while the rear wheels remain on the ground, the hand brake should be firmly ON. For most repair and replacement jobs under your vehicle these normal precautions will suffice. However, the vehicle needs to be even more stable than usual when carrying out these checks. There must be no risk of it toppling off its stands while suspension and steering components are being pushed and pulled in order to test them. Read carefully Chapter 1, Safety First! and the first part of Chapter 3, Servicing Your Car for further important information on raising and supporting a vehicle above the ground.

shoes for example. See *Chapter 3, Servicing Your Car* for information on how to check the brakes.

Buying And Selling

This chapter provides a procedure for checking your vehicle's condition prior to its official MoT test. The same procedure could be equally useful to UK and non-UK owners alike when examining vehicles prior to purchase (or sale for that matter). However, it must be emphasised that the official MoT certificate should not be regarded as any guarantee of the condition of a vehicle. All it proves is that the vehicle reached the required standards, in the opinion of a particular examiner, at the time and date it was tested.

Pass The MoT!

The aim of this chapter is to explain what is actually tested on a vehicle and (if it is not obvious) how the test is done. This should enable you to identify and eliminate problems before they undermine the safety or diminish the performance of your vehicle and long before they cause the expense and inconvenience of a test failure.

Tool Box

Dismantling apart, few tools are needed for testing. A light hammer is useful for tapping panels underneath the vehicle when looking for rust. If this produces a bright metallic noise, then the area being tapped is solid metal. If the noise produced is dull, the area contains rust or filler. When tapping sills and box sections, listen also for the sound of debris (that is, rust flakes) on the inside of the panel. Use a screwdriver to prod weak parts of panels. This may produce holes of course, but if the panels have rusted to that extent, you really ought to know about it. A strong lever (such as a tyre lever) can be useful for applying the required force to suspension joints etc. when assessing whether there is any wear in them.

You will need an assistant to operate controls and perhaps to wobble the road wheels while you inspect components under the vehicle.

Age Related Checks

Two more brief explanations are required before you start your informal test. Firstly, the age of the vehicle determines exactly which lights, seat belts and other items it should have. Frequently in the next few pages you will come across the phrase "Cars first used ..." followed by a date. A vehicle's "first used" date is either its date of first registration, or the date six months after it was manufactured, whichever was earlier. Or, if the vehicle was originally used without being registered (such as a vehicle which has been imported to the U.K. or an ex-H.M. Forces model, etc.) the "first used" date is the date of manufacture.

Rust And Load Bearing Areas

Secondly, there must not be excessive rust, serious distortion or any fractures affecting certain prescribed areas of the bodywork. These prescribed areas are load-bearing parts of the bodywork within 30 cm (12 in.) of anchorages or mounting points associated with testable items such as seat belts, brake pedal assemblies, master cylinders, servos, suspension and

steering components and also body mountings. Keep this rule in mind while inspecting the vehicle, but remember also that even if such damage occurs outside a prescribed area, it can cause failure of the test. Failure will occur if the damage is judged to reduce the continuity or strength of a main load-bearing part of the bodywork sufficiently to have an adverse effect on the braking or steering.

The following notes are necessarily abbreviated, and are for assistance only. They are not a definitive guide to all the MoT regulations. It is also worth mentioning that the varying degrees of discretion of individual MoT testers can mean that there are variations between the standards as applied. However, the following points should help to make you aware of the aspects which will be examined. Now, if you have your clipboard, checklist and pencil handy, let's make a start...

The 'Easy' Bits

Checking these items is straightforward and should not take more than a few minutes - and could avoid an embarrassingly simple failure...

Lights

Within the scope of the test are headlights, side and tail lights, brake lights, direction indicators, and number plate lights (plus rear fog lights on all cars first used on or after 1 April, 1980, and any earlier cars subsequently so equipped, and also hazard warning lights on any vehicle so fitted). All must operate, must be clean and not significantly damaged; flickering is also not permitted. The switches should also all work properly. Pairs of lights should give approximately the same intensity of light output, and operation of one set of lights should not affect the working of another - such trouble is usually due to bad earthing.

Front fog and spot lights are not part of the MoT test (although their use is covered by *Construction and Use* regulations so that, for instance, spot lights should go out when headlights are turned off main beam) and won't be tested, provided they're not a physical hazard. Rear fog lights are part of the Test however. See later in this Chapter for details.

Indicators should flash at between 60 and 120 times per minute. 'Rev' the engine to encourage them, if a little slow (although the examiner might not let you get away with it!) Otherwise, renew the (inexpensive) flasher unit and check all wiring and earth connections.

Interior 'tell-tale' lights, such as for indicators, rear fog lights and hazard warning lights should all operate in unison with their respective exterior lights.

Headlight aim must be correct - in particular, the lights should not dazzle other road users. An approximate guide can be obtained by shining the lights against a vertical wall, but final adjustment may be necessary by reference to the beam checking machine at the MoT station. Most testers will be happy to make slight adjustments where necessary but only if the adjusters work. Make sure before you take the vehicle in that they are not seized solid!

Reflectors must be unbroken, clean, and not obscured - for example, by stickers.

Wheels And Tyres

Check the wheels for loose nuts, cracks, and damaged rims. Missing wheel nuts or studs are also failure points, naturally enough!

There is no excuse for running on illegal tyres. The legal requirement is that there must be at least 1.6 mm of tread depth remaining, over the 'central' three-quarters of the width of the tyre all the way around. From this it can be deduced that there is no legal requirement to have 1.6 mm (1/16 in.) of tread on the 'shoulders' of the tyre, but in practice, most MoT stations will be reluctant to pass a tyre in this condition. In any case, for optimum safety - especially 'wet grip' - you would be well advised to change tyres when they wear down to around 3 mm (1/8 in.) or so depth of remaining tread.

Visible 'tread wear indicator bars', found approximately every nine inches around the tread of the tyre, are highlighted when the tread reaches the critical 1.6 mm point.

Tyres should not show signs of cuts or bulges, rubbing on the bodywork or running gear, and the valves should be in sound condition, and correctly aligned.

Old-fashioned cross-ply and radial-ply tyre types must not be mixed on the same axle, and if pairs of cross-ply and radial-ply tyres are fitted, the radials must be on the rear axle.

Windscreen

The screen must not be damaged (by cracks, chips, etc.) or obscured so that the driver does not have a clear view of the road. Permissible size of damage points depends on where they occur. Within an area 290 mm (nearly 12 in.) wide, ahead of the driver, and up to the top of the wiper arc, any damage must be confined within a circle less than 10 mm (approx. 0.4 in.) in diameter. This is increased to 40 mm (just over 1.5 in.) for damage within the rest of the screen area swept by the wipers.

Washers And Wipers

The wipers must clear an area big enough to give the driver a clear view forwards and to the side of the vehicle. The wiper blades must be securely attached and sound, with no cracks or 'missing' sections. The wiper switch should also work properly. The screen washers must supply the screen with sufficient liquid to keep it clean, in conjunction with the use of the wipers.

Mirrors

Your vehicle must have at least two, one of which must be on the driver's side. The mirrors must be visible from the driver's seat, and not be damaged or obscured so that the view to the rear is affected. Therefore cracks, chips and discolouration can mean failure.

Horn

The horn must emit a uniform note which is loud enough to give adequate warning of approach, and the switch must operate correctly. Multi-tone horns playing 'in sequence' are not permitted, but two tones sounding together are fine.

Seat Security

The seats must be securely mounted, and the sub-frames should be sound.

Seat Belts

Seat belts must be in good condition (i.e. not frayed or otherwise damaged), and the buckles and catches should also operate correctly. Inertia reel types, where fitted, should retract properly.

Belt mountings must be secure, with no structural damage or corrosion within 30 cm (12 in.) of them.

Number (Registration) Plates

Both front and rear number plates must be present, and in good condition, with no breaks or missing numbers or letters. The plates must not be obscured, and the digits must not be repositioned (to form names, for instance).

Vehicle Identification Numbers (VIN)

Vehicles first used on or after 1 August, 1980 have to have a clearly displayed VIN - Vehicle Identification Number (or old-fashioned 'chassis numbers' for older cars) which is plainly legible. See *Chapter 2, Buying Guide* for the correct location on your vehicle.

Exhaust System

The entire system must be present, properly mounted, free of leaks and should not be noisy - which can happen when the internal baffles fail. 'Proper' repairs by welding, or exhaust cement, or bandage are acceptable, as long as no gas leaks are evident. Then again, common sense, if not the MoT, dictates that exhaust bandage should only be a very short-term emergency measure. For safety's sake, fit a new exhaust if yours is reduced to this!

PART II: THE CHECKLIST

You've checked the easy bits - now it's time for the detail! Some of the 'easy bits' referred to above are included here, but this is intended as a more complete check list to give your vehicle the best possible chance of gaining a First Class Honours, MoT Pass!

Inside The Vehicle

☐ 1. The steering wheel should be examined for cracks and for damage which might interfere with its use, or injure the driver's hands. It should also be pushed and pulled along the column axis, and also up and down, at 90 degrees to it. This will highlight any deficiencies in the wheel and upper column mounting/bearing, and also any excessive end float, and movement between the column shaft and the wheel. Look, too, for movement in the steering column couplings and fasteners (including the universal joint if applicable), and visually check their condition and security. They must be sound, and properly tightened.

GETTING THROUGH THE MOT

In the case of cars (the majority) with steering racks, rotate the steering wheel in both directions to test for free play at the wheel rim - this shouldn't exceed approximately 13 mm. (0.5 in.), assuming a 380 mm. (15 in.) diameter steering wheel.

In the case of the smaller number of cars with steering boxes, free play at the wheel rim shouldn't exceed approximately 75 mm (3.0 in.), assuming a 380 mm (15 in.) diameter steering wheel.

In both cases where the steering wheel is larger or smaller the amount of permissible free play should be raised or lowered accordingly.

☐ 2. Check that the switches for headlights, sidelights, rear fog lights direction indicators, hazard warning lights, wipers, washers and horn, appear to be in good working order and check that the tell-tale lights or audible warnings are working where applicable.

☐ 3. Make sure that the windscreen wipers operate effectively with blades that are secure and in good condition. The windscreen washer should provide sufficient liquid to clear the screen in conjunction with the wipers.

☐ 4. Check for windscreen damage, especially in the area swept by the wipers. From the MoT tester's point of view, Zone A is part of this area, 290 mm (11.5 in.) wide and centred on the centre of the steering wheel. Damage to the screen within this area should be capable of fitting into a 10 mm (approx. 0.4 in.) diameter circle and the cumulative effect of more minor damage should not seriously restrict the driver's view. Windscreen stickers or other obstructions should not encroach more than 10 mm (approx 0.4 in.) into this area. In the remainder of the swept area the maximum diameter of damage or degree of encroachment by obstructions is 40 mm (approx. 1.6 in.) and there is no ruling regarding cumulative

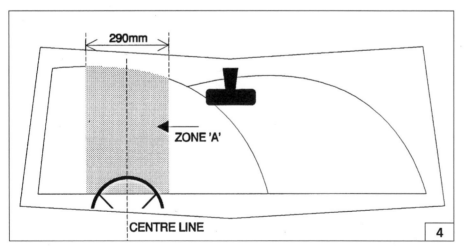

multi-tone horns (which alternate between two or more notes) are not permitted at all. On cars first used after 1 August 1973, the horn should produce a constant, continuous or uniform note which is neither harsh nor grating.

☐ 6. There must be one exterior mirror on the driver's side of the vehicle and one other mirror - either an exterior mirror fitted to the passenger's side or an interior mirror. The required mirrors should be secure and in good condition.

☐ 7. Check that the hand brake operates effectively without coming to the end of its working travel. The lever and its mechanism must be complete, securely mounted, unobstructed in its travel and in a sufficiently good condition to remain firmly in the "On" position even when knocked from side to side. The 30 cm rule on bodywork corrosion applies in the vicinity of the hand brake lever mounting.

☐ 8. The foot brake pedal assembly should be complete, unobstructed, and in a good working condition, including the pedal rubber (which should not have been worn smooth). There should be no excessive movement of the pedal at right angles to its normal direction. When fully depressed, the pedal should not be at the end of its travel. The pedal should not feel spongy (indicating air in the hydraulic system), nor should it tend to creep downwards while held under pressure (which indicates an internal hydraulic leak).

☐ 9. Seats must be secure on their mountings and seat backs must be capable of being locked in the upright position.

☐ 10. The law requires all models to be fitted with seatbelts for the driver and front passenger. These have to be three-point lap and diagonal belts. Rear seat belts are a requirement for vehicles first used after 31 March 1987 with three anchorage points for the 'outer' passengers, and at least a lap belt only for the centre passenger position. Examine seat belt webbing and fittings to make sure that all are in good condition and that anchorages are firmly attached to the vehicle's structure. Locking mechanisms should be capable of remaining locked, and of being released if required, when under load. Flexible buckle stalks (if fitted) should be free of corrosion, broken cable strands or other weaknesses. Note that any belts fitted which are not part of a legal requirements may be examined by the tester but will not form part of the official test.

damage. Specialist windscreen companies can often repair a cracked screen for a lot less than the cost of replacement. Moreover, the cost of repair is often covered by comprehensive insurance policies. DIY repair kits are also available.

☐ 5. The horn control should be present, secure and readily accessible to the driver, and the horn should be loud enough to be heard by other road users. Gongs, bells and sirens are not permitted (except as part of an anti-theft device) and

☐ 11. On inertia reel belts, check that on retracting the belts, the webbing winds into the retracting unit automatically, albeit with some manual assistance to start with.

☐ 12. Note the point raised earlier regarding corrosion around seat belt anchorage points. The MoT tester will not carry out any dismantling here, but he will examine floor mounted anchorage points from underneath the vehicle if that is possible.

GETTING THROUGH THE MOT

13. Before getting out of the vehicle, make sure that both doors can be opened from the inside.

Outside The Vehicle

14. Before closing the driver's door, check the condition of the inner sill. Usually the MoT tester will do this by applying finger or thumb pressure to various parts of the panel while the floor covering remains in place. For your own peace of mind, look beneath the sill covering, taking great care not to tear any covering. Then close the driver's door and make sure that it latches securely and repeat these checks on the nearside inner sill and door.

Now check all of the lights, front and rear, (and the number plate lights) while your assistant operates the light switches.

15. As we said earlier, you can carry out a rough and ready check on headlight alignment for yourself, although it will certainly not be as accurate as having it done for you at the MoT testing station. Drive your vehicle near to a wall, as shown. Check that your tyres are correctly inflated and the vehicle is on level ground.

Draw on the wall, with chalk:
• a horizontal line about 2 metres long, and at same height as centre of headlight lenses.
• two vertical lines about 1 metre long, each forming a cross with the horizontal line and the same distance apart as the headlight centres.
• another vertical line to form a cross on the horizontal line, midway between the others.

Now position your vehicle so that:
• it faces the wall squarely, and its centre line is in line with centre line marked on the wall.
• the steering is straight.
• headlight lenses are 5.0 metres (16 ft.) from the wall.

Switch on the headlights' 'main' and 'dipped' beams in turn and measure their centre points. You will be able to judge any major discrepancies in intensity and aim prior to having the beams properly set by a garage with beam measuring equipment.

Headlights should be complete, clean, securely mounted, in good working order and not adversely affected by the operation of another lamp, and these basic requirements affect all the lights listed below. Headlights must dip as a pair from a single switch. Their aim must be correctly adjusted and they should not be affected (even to the extent of flickering) when lightly tapped by hand. Each headlight should match its partner in terms of size, colour and intensity of light, and can be white or yellow.

16. Side lights should show white light to the front and red light to the rear. Lenses should not be broken, cracked or incomplete. Stop lights must be red, of course.

17. Check your indicators, doing what the MoT tester will do: turn on side lights and apply the brake lights while ensuring that the indicators still work properly, and that none of the lights interfere with each other, causing dimness or intermittent failure. Check side repeater lights, too.

18. Vehicles first used before 1 April 1986 do not have to have a hazard warning device, but if one is fitted, it must be tested, and it must operate with the ignition switch either on or off. The lights should flash 60-120 times per minute, and indicators must operate independently of any other lights.

19. There must be two red rear reflectors - always fitted by the manufacturers, of course! - which are clean and are securely and symmetrically fitted to the vehicle.

20. Your vehicle must have at least one rear fog light fitted to the centre or offside of the vehicle. If there are two, they must be spaced an equal distance from the centre. It must comply with the basic requirements (listed under headlights) and emit a steady red light. Its tell-tale light, inside the vehicle, must work to inform the driver that it is switched on.

21. There must be registration number plates at the front and rear of the vehicle and both must be clean, secure, complete and unobscured. Letters and figures must be correctly formed and correctly spaced and not likely to be misread due to an uncovered securing bolt or whatever. The year letter counts as a figure. The space between letters and figures must be at least twice that between adjacent letters or figures.

15

☐ 22. Number plate lights must be present, working, and must not flicker when tapped by hand, just as for other lights. Where more than one light or bulb was fitted as original equipment, all must be working.

Wheels And Tyres

The MoT tester will examine tyres and wheels while walking around the vehicle and again when he is underneath it.

☐ 23. Front tyres should match each other and rear tyres should match each other, both sets matching in terms of size, aspect ratio and type of structure. For example, you must never fit tyres of different sizes or types, such as cross-ply or radial, on the same 'axle' - both front wheels counting as 'on the same axle' in this context. If cross-ply or bias belted tyres are fitted to the rear of the car, you must not fit radial-ply tyres to the front. If cross-ply tyres are fitted to the rear, bias belted tyres should not be fitted to the front. (We recommend that you do not mix tyre types anywhere on the car.)

☐ 24. Failure of the test can be caused by a cut, lump, tear or bulge in a tyre, exposed ply or cord, a badly seated tyre, a re-cut tyre, a tyre fouling part of the vehicle, or a seriously damaged or misaligned valve stem which could cause sudden deflation of the tyre. To pass the test, the grooves of the tread pattern must be at least 1.6 mm deep throughout a continuous band comprising the central three-quarters of the breadth of tread, and round the entire outer circumference of the tyre.

We are grateful to Dunlop/SP Tyres for the photographs and information in this section.

☐ 24A. Modern tyres have tread wear indicators built into the tread groves (usually about eight of them spread equidistantly around the circumference). These appear as continuous bars running across the tread when the original pattern depth has worn down to 1.6 mm. There will be a distinct reduction in wet grip well before the tread wear indicators start to show, and you should replace tyres before they get to this stage, even though this is the legal minimum in the UK.

☐ 24B. Lumps and bulges in the tyre wall usually arise from accidental damage or even because of faults in the tyre construction. You should run your hand all the way around the side wall of the tyre, with the vehicle either jacked off the ground, or moving the vehicle half a wheels revolution, so that you can check the part of the tyre that was previously resting on the ground. Since you can't easily check the insides of the tyres in day-to-day use, it is even more important that you spend time carefully checking the inside of each tyre - the MoT tester will certainly do so! Tyres with bulges in them must be scrapped and replaced with new, since they can fail suddenly, causing your vehicle to lose control.

24B

24C

☐ 24C. Abrasion of the tyre side wall can take place either in conjunction with bulging, or by itself, and this invariably results from an impact, such as the tyre striking the edge of a kerb or a pothole in the road. Once again, the tyre may be at imminent risk of failure and you should take advice from a tyre specialist on whether the abrasion is just superficial, or whether the tyre will need replacement.

TWI

NEW TYRE   **ILLEGAL TYRE** 24A

☐ 24D. All tyres will suffer progressively from cracking, albeit in most cases superficially, due to the effects of sunlight. If old age has caused the tyres on your vehicle to degrade to this extent, replace them.

24D

☐ 24E. If the outer edges of the tread are worn noticeably more than the centre, the tyres have been run under inflated which not only ruins tyres, but causes worse fuel consumption, dangerous handling and is, of course, illegal.

Over-inflation causes the centre part of the tyre to wear more quickly than the outer edges. This is also illegal but in addition, it causes the steering and grip to suffer and the tyre becomes more susceptible to concussion damage.

24E

24F

☐ 24F. Incorrect wheel alignment causes one side of the tyre to wear more severely than the other. If your vehicle should hit a kerb or large pothole, it is worthwhile having the wheel alignment checked by a tyre specialist since this costs considerably less than new front tyres!

☐ 25. Road wheels must be secure and must not be badly damaged, distorted or cracked, or have badly distorted bead rims (perhaps due to "kerbing"), or loose or missing wheel nuts, studs or bolts.

☐ 26. Check the bodywork for any sharp edges or projections, caused by corrosion or damage, which could prove dangerous to other road users, including pedestrians.

☐ 27. Check that the fuel cap fastens securely and that its sealing washer is neither torn nor deteriorated, or its mounting flange damaged sufficiently to allow fuel to escape (for example, while the vehicle is cornering).

Under The Bonnet

☐ 28. The vehicle should have a Vehicle Identification Number fitted to the bodywork. This can be on a plate secured to the vehicle or, etched or stamped on the bodywork. See *Chapter 2, Buying Guide* for more information.

☐ 29. Check the steering rack or box for security by asking your assistant to turn the steering wheel from side to side (with the road wheels on the ground) while you watch what happens under the bonnet. Then, check for free play in the steering assembly as a whole. This is done by turning the steering wheel from side to side as far as possible without moving the road wheels - and measuring how far the steering wheel can be moved in this way. More than 75 mm (approx. 3 in.) of free play, on a steering box system, or 13 mm (approx. 0.5 in.), on a steering rack, at the perimeter of the steering wheel, due to wear in the steering components, is sufficient grounds for a test failure. Note that the free play is based on a steering wheel diameter of 380 mm (approx 15 in) and will be less for smaller steering wheels - which all of them virtually are! Also check for the presence and security of retaining and locking devices in the steering column assembly.

☐ 30. While peering under the bonnet, check that hydraulic master cylinders and reservoirs are securely mounted and not severely corroded or otherwise damaged. Ensure that the caps are present, that fluid levels are satisfactory and that there are no fluid leaks.

☐ 31. Also check that the brake servo is securely mounted and not damaged or corroded to an extent that would impair its operation. Vacuum pipes should be sound, that is, free from kinks, splits and excessive chafing and not collapsed internally.

☐ 32. Still under the bonnet have a thorough search for evidence of excessive corrosion, severe distortion or fracture in any load bearing panelling within 30 cm (12 in.) of important mounting points such as the master cylinder/servo mounting, front suspension mountings etc.

Under The Vehicle - Front End

> ☐ *33. SAFETY FIRST! On some occasions there is no alternative but for your assistant to sit in the vehicle whilst you go beneath. Therefore: 1) Place ramps as well as axle stands beneath the vehicle's structure so that it cannot fall. 2) Don't allow your assistant to move vigorously or get in or out of the vehicle while you are beneath it. If either of these are problematical, DON'T CARRY OUT CHECK 34 - leave it to your garage.*

☐ 34. Have an assistant turn the steering wheel from side to side while you watch for movement in the steering mechanism. Make sure that the rack or box mountings are secure, that the ball joints show no signs of wear and that the ball joint dust covers are in sound condition. Ensure that all split pins, locking nuts and so on are in place and correctly fastened, throughout the steering and suspension systems.

☐ 35. With each wheel raised in turn, spin the wheel listening for roughness in the bearings. There must be none.

☐ 36. Under the vehicle, check the condition of the front springs. Wearing goggles, use a stuff brush to clean off the mud and other debris so that you don't miss a hidden 'crack'. Make sure that all suspension mountings are sound.

☐ 37. Inspect the front shock absorbers. Their upper shrouds (outer casing) tend to rust. Any sign of leaks will cause failure of the test - look for weeping hydraulic fluid just below the lower edge of the upper shroud. Take a firm grip on the upper and lower shroud in turn with both hands and try to twist the damper to check for deterioration in the top and bottom mounting bushes.

☐ 38. With all four wheels on the ground, push down firmly a couple of times on each front wing of the vehicle, then let go at the bottom of the stroke. The vehicle should return to approximately its original level within two or three strokes. Continuing oscillations will earn your vehicle a 'failure' ticket for worn front shockers!

Under The Vehicle - Rear Suspension

☐ 39. Check the operation of the rear shock absorbers in the same way as the front (Check 38).

☐ 40. Check the rear wheel bearings as described in check 35.

☐ 41. Check the condition of the rear springs and suspension components as described in check 36.

☐ 42. Check the condition of the rear shock absorbers as described in check 37.

Braking System

☐ 43. The MoT brake test is carried out on a special 'rolling road' set-up, which measures the efficiency in terms of percentage. For the foot brake, the examiner is looking for 50 per cent; the hand brake must measure 25 per cent. Frankly, without a rolling road of your own, there is little that you can do to verify whether or not your vehicle will come up to the required figures. What you can do, though, is carry out an entire check of the brake system, which will also cover all other aspects the examiner will be checking, and be as sure as you can that the system is working efficiently.

IMPORTANT! See *Chapter 3, Servicing Your Car* for important information, including *SAFETY FIRST!* information before working on your vehicle's brakes.

☐ 44. The MoT examiner will not dismantle any part of the system, but you can do so. So, take off each front wheel in turn, and examine as follows:

Disc Brakes

Check the front brake discs themselves, looking for excessive grooving or crazing, the calliper pistons/dust seals (looking for signs of fluid leakage and deterioration of the seals), and the brake pads - ideally, replace them if less than approximately 3mm (1/8th in.) friction material remains on each pad - but check the recommendations in *Chapter 3*.

Drum Brakes

Remove each brake drum and check the condition of the linings (renew if worn down to anywhere near the rivet heads), the brake drum (watch for cracking, ovality and serious scoring, etc.) and the wheel cylinders. Check the cylinder's dust covers to see if they contain brake fluid. If so, or if it is obvious that the cylinder(s) have been leaking, replace them or - ONLY if the cylinder bore is in perfect condition - fit a new seal kit.

☐ 45. Ensure that the drum brake adjusters (where fitted) are free to rotate (i.e. not seized!). If they are stuck fast, apply a little penetrating oil (but if possible, only from behind the backplate; if you have to work inside the brake drum, take great care to avoid the risk of getting oil on the brake shoes), and gently work the adjuster backwards and forwards with a brake adjuster spanner. Eventually the adjusters should free and a little brake grease can be applied to the threads to keep them in this condition. Now rotate the adjuster until the brake shoes contact the drum (preventing the road wheel from turning), then reverse the adjustment just enough to allow the wheel to turn.

☐ 46. A similar procedure can be applied to the handbrake adjustment. Check that the handbrake applies the brakes fully, well before it reaches the end of its potential range of movement. Ensure that the handbrake lever remains locked in the 'on' position when fully applied, even if the lever is knocked sideways.

☐ 47. Closely check the state of ALL visible hydraulic pipework. If any section of the steel tubing shows signs of corrosion, replace it, for safety as well as to gain an MoT pass. Look too for leakage of fluid around pipe joints, and from the master cylinder. The fluid level in the master cylinder reservoir must also be at its correct level - if not, find out why and rectify the problem! At the front and rear of the vehicle, bend the flexible hydraulic pipes (by hand) near each end of each pipe, checking for signs of cracking. If any is evident, or if the pipes have been chafing on the tyres, wheels, steering or suspension components, replace them with new items, rerouting them to avoid future problems. Note also that where the manufacturers fitted a clip to secure a piece of pipe, then it must be present and the pipe must be secured by it.

☐ 48. Have an assistant press down hard on the brake pedal while you check all flexible pipes for bulges. As an additional check, firmly apply the foot brake and hold the pedal down for a few minutes. It should not slowly sink to the floor (if it does, you have a hydraulic system problem). Press and release the pedal a few times - it should not feel 'spongy' (due to the presence of air in the system). Now check the operation of the brake servo by starting the engine while the brake pedal is being held down. If all is well, as the vacuum servo starts to work, the pedal should move a short distance towards the floor. Check the condition of the servo unit and its hoses - all MUST be sound. If there is the risk of any problems with the braking system's hydraulics, have a qualified mechanic check it over before using the vehicle.

☐ 49. A test drive should reveal obvious faults (such as pulling to one side, due to a seized calliper piston, for example), but otherwise all will be revealed on the rollers at the MoT station...

Bodywork Structure

A structurally deficient vehicle is a dangerous vehicle, and rust can affect many important areas, including the sills, any 'outriggers' and the floorpan. Examine these areas carefully.

☐ 50. Essentially, fractures, cracks or serious corrosion in any load bearing panel or member (to the extent that the affected sections are weakened) need to be dealt with. In addition, failure will result from any deficiencies in the structural metalwork within 30 cm (12 in.) of the seat belt mountings, and also the steering and suspension component attachment points. Repairs made to any structural areas must be carried out by 'continuous' seam welding, and the repair should restore the affected section to at least its original strength.

☐ 51. The MoT examiner will be looking for metal which gives way under squeezing pressure between finger and thumb, and will use his wicked little 'Corrosion Assessment Tool' (i.e. a plastic-headed tool known as the 'toffee hammer'!), which in theory at least should be used for detecting rust by lightly tapping the surface. If scraping the surface of the metal shows weakness beneath, the vehicle will fail.

☐ 52. Note that the security of doors and other openings must also be assessed, including the hinges, locks and catches. Corrosion damage or other weakness in the vicinity of these

items can mean failure. All doors must latch securely. It must be possible to open both front doors from inside and outside the vehicle and rear doors from the outside only.

Exterior Bodywork

☐ 53. Look out for surface rust, or accident damage, on the exterior bodywork, which leaves sharp/jagged edges and which may be liable to cause injury. Ideally, repairs should be carried out by welding in new metal, but for non-structural areas, riveting a plate over a hole, bridging the gap with glass fibre/body filler or even taping over the gap can be legally acceptable, at least as far as the MoT test is concerned.

Fuel System

☐ 54. Another recent extension of the regulations brings the whole of the fuel system under scrutiny, from the tank to the engine. The system should be examined with and without the engine running, and there must be no leaks from any of the components. The tank must be securely mounted, and the filler cap must fit properly - 'temporary' caps are not permitted.

Emissions

☐ 55. In almost every case, a proper 'engine tune' will help to ensure that your vehicle is running at optimum efficiency, and there should be no difficulty in passing the test, unless your engine or its ancillaries are well worn.

All petrol engines are subject to the 'visual smoke emission' test. The engine must be fully warmed up, allowed to idle, then revved slightly. If smoke emitted is regarded by the examiner as being 'excessive', the vehicle will fail. Often smoke emitted during this test is as a result of worn valve stem seals, allowing oil into the combustion chambers during tickover, to be blown out of the exhaust as 'blue smoke' when the engine is revved. In practice, attitudes vary widely between MoT stations on this aspect of the test.

☐ 56. For diesel-engined vehicles a 'smoke' test also applies. Again, the engine must be fully warmed up, and allowed to idle, before being revved to around 2,500 rpm for 20 seconds (to 'purge' the system). If dense blue or black smoke is emitted for more than five seconds, the vehicle will fail. In addition, the exhaust smoke is tested. Problems will require **SPECIALIST SERVICE.**

GETTING THROUGH THE MOT

FACT FILE: VEHICLE EMISSIONS

PETROL ENGINED VEHICLES WITHOUT CATALYSER

Vehicles first used before 1 August 1973
• visual smoke check only.

Vehicles first used between 1 August 1973 and 31 July 1986
• 4.5% carbon monoxide and 1,200 parts per million, unburned hydrocarbons.

Vehicles first used between 1 August 1986 and 31 July 1992
• 3.5% carbon monoxide and 1,200 parts per million, unburned hydrocarbons.

PETROL ENGINED VEHICLES FITTED WITH CATALYTIC CONVERTERS

**Vehicles first used from 1 August 1992
(K-registration on).**

All have to be tested at an MoT Testing Station specially equipped to handle cars fitted with catalytic converters whether or not the vehicle is fitted with a 'cat'. If the test, or the garage's data, shows that the vehicle was not fitted with a 'cat' by the manufacturer, the owner is permitted to take the vehicle to a Testing Station not equipped for catalysed cars, if he/she prefers to do so (up to 1998-only). Required maxima are - 3.5% carbon monoxide and 1,200 parts per million, unburned hydrocarbons. The simple emissions test (as above) will be supplemented by a further check to make sure that the catalyst is maintained in good and efficient working order.

The tester also has to check that the engine oil is up to a specified temperature before carrying out the test. (This is because 'carbs' don't work properly at lower temperatures - ensure *your* engine is fully warm!)

DIESEL ENGINES' EMISSIONS STANDARDS

The Tester will have to rev your engine hard, several times. If it is not in good condition, he is entitled to refuse to test it. This is the full range of tests, even though all may not apply to your car.

Vehicles first used before 1 August, 1979

Engine run at normal running temperature; engine speed taken to around 2500 rpm (or half governed max. speed, if lower) and held for 20 seconds. FAILURE, if engine emits dense blue or black smoke for next 5 seconds, at tick-over. (NOTE: Testers are allowed to be more lenient with pre-1960 vehicles.)

Vehicles first used on or after 1 August, 1979

After checking engine condition, and with the engine at normal running temperature, the engine will be run up to full revs between three and six times to see whether your engine passes the prescribed smoke density test. (For what it's worth - 2.5k for non-turbo cars; 3.0k for turbo diesels. An opacity meter probe will be placed in your car's exhaust pipe and this is not something you can replicate at home.) Irrespective of the meter readings, the car will fail if smoke or vapour obscures the view of other road users.

IMPORTANT NOTE: The diesel engine test puts a lot of stress on the engine. It is IMPERATIVE that your car's engine is properly serviced, and the cam belt changed on schedule, before you take it in for the MoT test. The tester is entitled to refuse to test the car if he feels that the engine is not in serviceable condition and there are a number of pre-Test checks he may carry out.

CHAPTER 8 - FACTS & FIGURES

PART I - MAJOR MILESTONES

Sept. 1983 - 205 introduced in 5-door body style only. Petrol engines designated XV, XW and XY, all with chain-driven over-head camshaft in capacities of 954cc, 1124cc and 1360cc respectively. The 4 or 5 speed gearbox formed an integral part of the engine block, being placed beneath the crankcase and sharing lubrication with the engine. Diesel engine available in XUD 1700cc form, with separate gearbox. Various trim options available over whole range.

Apr. 1984 - GTI model introduced with 1580cc XU5-type engine using a belt-driven camshaft, separate 5 speed gearbox and alloy wheels as standard, in a new 3-door hatchback body style.

Oct. 1984 - Three door body style made available in all configurations (not just GTI) and all such models designated 'X' series.

June 1985 - Van bodied model introduced with option of petrol or diesel engine.

Apr. 1986 - Automatic transmission introduced as option, but only available with 1580cc engine. Cabriolet CTI also introduced, fitted with single-point fuel-injected 1580cc XU5 engine. GTI engine uprated to 115 BHP.

Sept. 1986 - Launch of 1905cc XU9 engine fitted to GTI, replacing smaller XU5 unit (not available in UK until January 1987) along with rear disc brakes and modified 'sports' suspension.

Dec. 1987 - Range revised, changes including uprated 1.0, 1.1 and 1.4 litre engines designated 'TU', new MA-type 5-speed gearbox introduced for whole range except fuel-injected, diesel and automatic models.

June 1988 - 1.4 litre Cabriolet introduced, designated CJ, with carburettor equipped engine.

Aug. 1990 - 1.6 litre Cabriolet now fitted with electric hood (optional on 1.4 litre).

Oct. 1991 - 1.8 litre turbo-diesel engine introduced, but only in three-door body style; Cabriolet versions now fitted with catalytic converter - also available on 1.1 and 1.4 litre fuel-injected engines.

June 1994 - Special 3- and 5-door 'Mardi Gras' editions launched in 1.1, 1.6 Auto., 1.8 diesel and turbo-diesel types.

Sept. 1994 - Mardi Gras models now adopted as standard range.

Aug. 1995 - All models begin phasing out, but still available into 1996.

Dec. 1995 - Model officially discontinued. Some 1996 vehicles registered.

FACTS & FIGURES

PART II - CAPACITIES AND SETTINGS

1.0 litre Petrol - 1983 to 88
Engine type - XV8
Firing order - 1,3,4,2
Cubic capacity - 954cc
Compression ratio - 9.3:1
Carburettor type - SOLEX 32 PBSIA 12
Idle speed - 650 RPM
CO percentage - 0.8 TO 1.5
Spark plug type - H7DC
Spark plug gap - 0.6 mm (0.024 in.)
Ignition timing (at idle) - 6 DEG.
Valve clearances - inlet - 0.10 mm (0.15 mm FROM 1987)
outlet - 0.25 mm (0.30 mm FROM 1987)
Cooling system pressure cap setting - 0.8 bar (11.6 lbf/sq in.)
Fuses - see *Fuses Fact File in Chapter 3, p26.*
Brake disc thickness - 10.0 mm
minimum disc thickness - 8.5 mm
minimum pad thickness - 2.0 mm
Brake drum internal diameter - 180.0 mm
Brake drum internal diameter after resurfacing - 181.0 mm
minimum brake shoe thickness - 1.0 mm
Torque wrench setting:
Spark plugs - 15-20 Nm
Wheel bolts - 85 Nm

1.0 litre Petrol - 1988 to 1992
Engine type - TU
Firing order - 1,3,4,2
Cubic capacity - 954cc
Compression ratio - 9.4:1
Carburettor type - Solex/Weber 32 BISA16/32 1BSH16
Idle speed - 700 rpm
CO percentage - 0.5 to 1.0
Spark plug type - F7DCOR
Spark plug gap - 0.8 mm (0.032 in.)
Ignition timing - 8 deg. BTDC
Valve clearances: - inlet - 0.20 mm
outlet - 0.40 mm
Cooling system pressure cap setting - 0.8 bar (11.6 lbf/sq in.)
Fuses - see *Fuses Fact File in Chapter 3, p26.*
Brake disc thickness - 10.0 mm
minimum disc thickness - 8.5 mm
minimum pad thickness - 2.0 mm
Brake drum internal diameter - 180.0 mm
Brake drum internal diameter after resurfacing - 181.0 mm
minimum brake shoe thickness - 1.0 mm
Torque wrench setting:
Spark plugs - 18 Nm
Wheel bolts - 85 Nm

1.1 litre Petrol - 1983 to '88
Engine type - XW7
Firing order - 1,3,4,2
Cubic capacity - 1124cc
Compression ratio - 9.7:1
Carburettor type - Solex 32 PBISA
Idle speed - 650 rpm
CO percentage - 1.5%
Spark plug type - H7DC
Spark plug gap - 0.6 mm (0.024 in.)

Ignition timing - 6 deg.BTDC
Valve clearances: - inlet - 0.10 mm
outlet - 0.25 mm
Cooling system pressure cap setting - 0.8 bar (11.6 lbf/sq in.)
Fuses - see *Fuses Fact File in Chapter 3, p26.*
Brake disc thickness - 10.0 mm
minimum disc thickness - 8.5 mm
minimum pad thickness - 2.0 mm
Brake drum internal diameter - 180.0 mm
Brake drum internal diameter after resurfacing - 181.0 mm
minimum brake shoe thickness - 1.0 mm
Torque wrench setting:
Spark plugs - 18 Nm
Wheel bolts - 85 Nm

1.1 litre Petrol - 1988 to '92
Engine type - TU1
Firing order - 1,3,4,2
Cubic capacity - 1124 cc
Compression ratio - 9.4:1
Carburettor type - Solex 32 PBISA16
Idle speed - 850 rpm
CO percentage - 0.5 to 1.0 %
Spark plug type - F7DCOR
Spark plug gap - 0.8 mm (0.032 in.)
Ignition timing - 8 deg. BTDC
Valve clearances: - inlet - 0.20 mm
outlet - 0.40 mm
Cooling system pressure cap setting - 0.8 bar (11.6 lbf/sq in.)
Fuses - see *Fuses Fact File in Chapter 3, p26.*
Brake disc thickness - 10.0 mm
minimum disc thickness - 8.5 mm
minimum pad thickness - 2.0 mm
Brake drum internal diameter - 180.0 mm
Brake drum internal diameter after resurfacing - 181.0 mm
minimum brake shoe thickness - 1.0 mm
Torque wrench setting:
Spark plugs - 18 Nm
Wheel bolts - 85 Nm

1.1 litre Petrol (With Catalyst) - 1989 to '92
Engine type - TU1M
Firing order - 1,3,4,2
Cubic capacity - 1124 cc
Compression ratio - 9.4:1
Fuel injection type - Mono-Jetronic
Idle speed - 850 rpm
CO percentage - 0.4 (max)
Spark plug type - RFC42LS
Spark plug gap - 0.8 mm (0.032 in.)
Ignition timing - 8 deg BTDC at 900 rpm
Valve clearances: - inlet - 0.20 mm
outlet - 0.40 mm
Cooling system pressure cap setting - 0.8 bar (11.6 lbf/sq in.)
Fuses - see *Fuses Fact File in Chapter 3, p26.*
Brake disc thickness - 10.0 mm
minimum disc thickness - 8.5 mm
minimum pad thickness - 2.0 mm
Brake drum internal diameter - 180.0 mm
Brake drum internal diameter after resurfacing - 181.0 mm

minimum brake shoe thickness - 1.0 mm
Torque wrench setting:
Spark plugs - 18 Nm
Wheel bolts - 85 Nm

1.4 litre Petrol - 1983 to '87
Engine type - XY7
Firing order - 1,3,4,2
Cubic capacity - 1360 cc
Compression ratio - 9.3:1
Carburettor type - SOLEX 34 PBISA
Idle speed - 650 rpm
CO percentage - 1.5%
Spark plug type - H7DC
Spark plug gap - 0.6 mm (0.024 in.)
Ignition timing - 8 Deg. BTDC @ 650 rpm
Valve clearances: - inlet - 0.10 mm
outlet - 0.25 mm
Cooling system pressure cap setting - 0.8 bar (11.6 lbf/sq in.)
Fuses - see *Fuses Fact File in Chapter 3, p26.*
Brake disc thickness - 10.0 mm
minimum disc thickness - 8.5 mm
minimum pad thickness - 2.0 mm
Brake drum internal diameter - 180.0 mm
Brake drum internal diameter after resurfacing - 181.0 mm
minimum brake shoe thickness - 1.0 mm
Torque wrench setting:
Spark plugs - 18 Nm
Wheel bolts - 85 Nm

1.4 litre Petrol - 1983 to '87
Engine Type - XY8
Firing order - 1,3,4,2
Cubic capacity - 1360 cc
Compression ratio - 9.3:1
Carburettor type - SOLEX 35 PBISA8
Idle speed - 950 rpm
CO percentage - 2.0%
Spark plug type - H6DC
Spark plug gap - 0.6 mm (0.024 in.)
Ignition timing - 8 Deg. BTDC @ 850 rpm
Valve clearances: - inlet - 0.10 mm
outlet - 0.25 mm
Cooling system pressure cap setting - 0.8 bar (11.6 lbf/sq in.)
Fuses - see *Fuses Fact File in Chapter 3, p26.*
Brake disc thickness - 10.0 mm
minimum disc thickness - 8.5 mm
minimum pad thickness - 2.0 mm
Brake drum internal diameter - 180.0 mm
Brake drum internal diameter after resurfacing - 181.0 mm
minimum brake shoe thickness - 1.0 mm
Torque wrench setting:
Spark plugs - 18 Nm
Wheel bolts - 85 Nm

1.4 litre Petrol - 1987 to '88
Engine type - TU3
Firing order - 1,3,4,2
Cubic capacity - 1360 cc
Compression ratio - 9.3:1
Carburettor type - Weber 34 TLP3
Idle speed - 750 rpm
CO percentage - 0.8 to 1.5 %

Spark plug type - F7DCOR
Spark plug gap - 0.8 mm (0.032 in.)
Ignition timing - 8 deg BTDC
Valve clearances: - inlet - 0.20 mm
outlet - 0.40 mm
Cooling system pressure cap setting - 0.8 bar
(11.6 lbf/sq in.)
Fuses - see *Fuses Fact File in Chapter 3, p26.*
Brake disc thickness - 10.0 mm
minimum disc thickness - 8.5 mm
minimum pad thickness - 2.0 mm
Brake drum internal diameter - 180.0 mm
Brake drum internal diameter after resurfacing
- 181.0 mm
minimum brake shoe thickness - 1.0 mm
Torque wrench setting:
Spark plugs - 18 Nm
Wheel bolts - 85 Nm

1.4 litre Petrol - 1988 to '90
Engine type - TU3S
Firing order - 1,3,4,2
Cubic capacity - 1360 cc
Compression ratio - 9.3:1
Carburettor type - Solex 34 34 32
Idle speed - 750 rpm
CO percentage - 1.0%
Spark plug type - FC58LS
Spark plug gap - 0.8 mm (0.032 in.)
Ignition timing - 8 deg. BTDC (4 deg. if
unleaded fuel used)
Valve clearances: - inlet - 0.20 mm
outlet - 0.40 mm
Cooling system pressure cap setting - 0.8 bar
(11.6 lbf/sq in.)
Fuses - see *Fuses Fact File in Chapter 3, p26.*
Brake disc thickness - 10.0 mm
minimum disc thickness - 8.5 mm
minimum pad thickness - 2.0 mm
Brake drum internal diameter - 180.0 mm
Brake drum internal diameter after resurfacing
- 181.0 mm
minimum brake shoe thickness - 1.0 mm
Torque wrench setting:
Spark plugs - 18 Nm
Wheel bolts - 85 Nm

1.4 litre Petrol - 1988 to '92
Engine type - TU3A
Firing order - 1,3,4,2
Cubic capacity - 1360 cc
Compression ratio - 9.3:1
Carburettor type - Solex 34 PBISA 17
Idle speed - 800 rpm
CO percentage - 0.8 to 1.5 %
Spark plug type - F7DCOR
Spark plug gap - 0.8 mm (0.032 in.)
Ignition timing - 8 deg. BTDC @ 750 rpm
Valve clearances: - inlet - 0.20 mm
outlet - 0.40 mm
Cooling system pressure cap setting - 0.8 bar
(11.6 lbf/sq in.)
Fuses - see *Fuses Fact File in Chapter 3, p26.*
Brake disc thickness - 10.0 mm
minimum disc thickness - 8.5 mm
minimum pad thickness - 2.0 mm
Brake drum internal diameter - 180.0 mm
Brake drum internal diameter after resurfacing
- 181.0 mm
minimum brake shoe thickness - 1.0 mm

Torque wrench setting:
Spark plugs - 18 Nm
Wheel bolts - 85 Nm

1.4 litre Petrol (Catalyst) - 1991 to '93
Engine type - TU3MIZ
Firing order - 1,3,4,2
Cubic capacity - 1360 cc
Compression ratio - 9.3:1
Fuel injection type - Bosch Mono-Jetronic A2.2
Idle speed - 850 rpm
CO percentage - 0.4 (max)
Spark plug type - RFC52LS
Spark plug gap - 0.8 mm (0.032 in.)
Ignition timing - 8 deg. BTDC @900 rpm
Valve clearances: - inlet - 0.20 mm
outlet - 0.40 mm
Cooling system pressure cap setting - 0.8 bar
(11.6 lbf/sq in.)
Fuses - see *Fuses Fact File in Chapter 3, p26.*
Brake disc thickness - 10.0 mm
minimum disc thickness - 8.5 mm
minimum pad thickness - 2.0 mm
Brake drum internal diameter - 180.0 mm
Brake drum internal diameter after resurfacing
- 181.0 mm
minimum brake shoe thickness - 1.0 mm
Torque wrench setting:
Spark plugs - 18 Nm
Wheel bolts - 85 Nm

1.6 litre Petrol - 1986 to '91
Engine type - XU51C
Firing order - 1,3,4,2
Cubic capacity - 1580 cc
Compression ratio - 9.35:1
Carburettor type - Weber 36 TLC1
Idle speed - 750 rpm
CO percentage - 1.0 %
Spark plug type - C62LJS
Spark plug gap - 0.60 mm (0.024 in.)
Ignition timing - 10 deg BTDC
Valve clearances: - inlet - 0.20 mm
outlet - 0.40 mm
Cooling system pressure cap setting - 0.8 bar
(11.6 lbf/sq in.)
Fuses - see *Fuses Fact File in Chapter 3, p26.*
Brake disc thickness - 10.0 mm
minimum disc thickness - 8.5 mm
minimum pad thickness - 2.0 mm
Brake drum internal diameter - 180.0 mm
Brake drum internal diameter after resurfacing
- 181.0 mm
minimum brake shoe thickness - 1.0 mm
Torque wrench setting:
Spark plugs - 18 Nm
Wheel bolts - 85 Nm

1.6 litre Petrol - 1991 to '93
Engine type - XU51C
Firing order - 1,3,4,2
Cubic capacity - 1580 cc
Compression ratio - 9.35:1
Carburettor type - Weber 36 TLC20
Idle speed - 750 rpm
CO percentage - 1.0 %
Spark plug type - FC58LS
Spark plug gap - 0.8 mm (0.032 in.)
Ignition timing - 10 deg BTDC
Valve clearances: - inlet - 0.20 mm
outlet - 0.40 mm

Cooling system pressure cap setting - 0.8 bar
(11.6 lbf/sq in.)
Fuses - see *Fuses Fact File in Chapter 3, p26.*
Brake disc thickness - 10.0 mm
minimum disc thickness - 8.5 mm
minimum pad thickness - 2.0 mm
Brake drum internal diameter - 180.0 mm
Brake drum internal diameter after resurfacing
- 181.0 mm
minimum brake shoe thickness - 1.0 mm
Torque wrench setting:
Spark plugs - 18 Nm
Wheel bolts - 85 Nm

1.6 litre Petrol (Catalyst) - 1991 to '93
Engine type - XU5M3Z
Firing order - 1,3,4,2
Cubic capacity - 1580 cc
Compression ratio - 9.35:1
Fuel injection type - Solex MMBAG5
Idle speed - 850 rpm (non-adjustable)
CO percentage - not adjustable
Spark plug type - FC52LS
Spark plug gap - 0.8 mm (0.032 in.)
Ignition timing - Pre-set (computer controlled)
Valve clearances: - inlet - 0.20 mm
outlet - 0.40 mm
Cooling system pressure cap setting - 0.8 bar
(11.6 lbf/sq in.)
Fuses - see *Fuses Fact File in Chapter 3, p26.*
Brake disc thickness - 10.0 mm
minimum disc thickness - 8.5 mm
minimum pad thickness - 2.0 mm
Brake drum internal diameter - 181.0 mm
Brake drum internal diameter after resurfacing
- 181.0 mm
minimum brake shoe thickness - 1.0 mm
Torque wrench setting:
Spark plugs - 18 Nm
Wheel bolts - 85 Nm

1.6 litre GTI - 1984 to '87
Engine type - XU5J
Firing order - 1,3,4,2
Cubic capacity - 1580 cc
Compression ratio - 9.8:1
Fuel injection type - Bosch LE2 Jetronic
Idle speed - 900 rpm
CO percentage - 1.0 &
Spark plug type - H6DC
Spark plug gap - 0.60 mm (0.024 in.)
Ignition timing - 6 deg BTDC @ 700 rpm
Valve clearances: - inlet - 0.20 mm
outlet - 0.40 mm
Cooling system pressure cap setting - 1.0 bar
(14.5 lbf/sq in.)
Fuses - see *Fuses Fact File in Chapter 3, p26.*
Brake disc thickness - 20.4 mm (ventilated)
minimum disc thickness - 18.9 mm
minimum pad thickness - 2.0 mm
Brake drum internal diameter - 180.0 mm
Brake drum internal diameter after resurfacing
- 181.0 mm
minimum brake shoe thickness - 1.0 mm
Torque wrench setting:
Spark plugs - 18 Nm
Wheel bolts - 85 Nm

1.6 litre Petrol GTI & CTI - 1987 to '93
Engine type - XU5JA
Firing order - 1,3,4,2

Cubic capacity - 1580 cc
Compression ratio - 9.8:1
Fuel injection type - Bosch LE2 Jetronic
Idle speed - 900 rpm
CO percentage - 1.0%
Spark plug type - S279YC
Spark plug gap - 0.8 mm (0.032 in.)
Ignition timing - 10 deg BTDC
Valve clearances: - inlet - 0.20 mm
outlet - 0.40 mm
Cooling system pressure cap setting - 1.0 bar
(14.5 lbf/sq in.)
Fuses - see *Fuses Fact File in Chapter 3, p26.*
Brake disc thickness - 20.4 mm (ventilated)
minimum disc thickness - 18.9 mm
minimum pad thickness - 2.0 mm
Brake drum internal diameter - 180.0 mm
Brake drum internal diameter after resurfacing -
181.0 mm
minimum brake shoe thickness - 1.0 mm
Torque wrench setting:
Spark plugs - 18 Nm
Wheel bolts - 85 Nm

1.9 litre Petrol GTI - 1987 to '93
Engine type - XU9 JA
Firing order - 1,3,4,2
Cubic capacity - 1905 cc
Compression ratio - 9.6:1
Fuel injection type - Bosch LU2 Jetronic
Idle speed - 900 rpm
CO percentage - 0.5 %
Spark plug type - FC58LS
Spark plug gap - 0.8 mm (0.032 in.)
Ignition timing - 5 deg BTDC @ 700 rpm
Valve clearances: - inlet - 0.20 mm
outlet - 0.40 mm
Cooling system pressure cap setting - 0.8 bar
(11.6 lbf/sq in.)
Fuses - see *Fuses Fact File in Chapter 3, p26.*
Brake disc thickness - 20.4 mm (ventilated)
minimum disc thickness - 18.9 mm
minimum pad thickness - 2.0 mm
Brake drum internal diameter - 180.0 mm
Brake drum internal diameter after resurfacing -
181.0 mm
minimum brake shoe thickness - 1.0 mm
Torque wrench setting:
Spark plugs - 18 Nm
Wheel bolts - 85 Nm

1.9 litre Petrol GTI (Catalyst) - 1990 to '93
Engine type - XU9 JAL
Firing order - 1,3,4,2
Cubic capacity - 1905 cc
Compression ratio - 9.2:1
Fuel injection type - Bosch MI3 Motronic
Idle speed - 900 rpm
CO percentage - 0.5 % (max)
Spark plug type - RFC52LS
Spark plug gap - 0.8 mm (0.032 in.)
Ignition timing - Preset, computer controlled
Valve clearances: - inlet - 0.20 mm
outlet - 0.40 mm
Cooling system pressure cap setting - 0.8 bar
(11.6 lbf/sq in.)
Fuses - see *Fuses Fact File in Chapter 3, p26.*
Brake disc thickness - 20.4 mm (ventilated)
minimum disc thickness - 18.9 mm

minimum pad thickness - 2.0 mm
Brake drum internal diameter - 180.0 mm
Brake drum internal diameter after resurfacing -
181.0 mm
minimum brake shoe thickness - 1.0 mm
Torque wrench setting:
Spark plugs - 30 Nm
Wheel bolts - 85 Nm

1.9 litre Petrol CTI - 1991 to '95
Engine type - XU9 JI/L/Z
Firing order - 1,3,4,2
Cubic capacity - 1905 cc
Compression ratio - 8.4:1
Fuel injection type - Bosch LU.2 Jetronic
Idle speed - 850 to 900 rpm
CO percentage - not adjustable
Spark plug type - RFC 52LS
Spark plug gap - 0.8 mm (0.032 in.)
Ignition timing - 10 deg BTDC
Valve clearances: - inlet - 0.20 mm
outlet - 0.40 mm
Cooling system pressure cap setting - 0.8 bar
(11.6 lbf/sq in.)
Fuses - see *Fuses Fact File in Chapter 3, p26.*
Brake disc thickness - 20.4 (ventilated)
minimum disc thickness - 18.9 mm
minimum pad thickness - 2.0 mm
Brake drum internal diameter - 180.0 mm
Brake drum internal diameter after resurfacing -
181.0 mm
minimum brake shoe thickness - 1.0 mm
Torque wrench setting:
Spark plugs - 27 Nm
Wheel bolts - 85 Nm

1.8 litre Diesel - 1983 to '95
Engine type - XUD7
Firing order - 1,3,4,2
Cubic capacity - 1769 cc
Compression ratio - 23:1
Fuel injection type - Bosch
Idle speed - 800 +/- 50 rpm
Glow plug type - CH 68
Valve clearances: - inlet - 0.15 mm
outlet - 0.30 mm
Cooling system pressure cap setting - 1.0 bar
(14.5 lbf/sq in.)
Fuses - see *Fuses Fact File in Chapter 3, p26.*
Brake disc thickness -
minimum disc thickness -
minimum pad thickness -
Brake drum internal diameter - 180.0 mm
Brake drum internal diameter after resurfacing -
181.0 mm
minimum brake shoe thickness - 1.0 mm
Torque wrench setting:
Glow plugs - 2,5m.daN (18 lbf.ft.)
Wheel bolts - 85 Nm

1.8 litre Diesel Turbo - 1990 to '95
Engine type - XUD7D T/L
Firing order - 1,3,4,2
Cubic capacity - 1769 cc
Compression ratio - 22:1
Fuel injection type - Roto-Diesel
Idle speed - 750 to 800 rpm
Glow plug type - CH 68
Valve clearances: - inlet - 0.15 mm
outlet - 0.30 mm

Cooling system pressure cap setting - 1.0 bar
(14.5 lbf/sq in.)
Fuses - see *Fuses Fact File in Chapter 3, p26.*
Brake disc thickness -
minimum disc thickness -
minimum pad thickness -
Brake drum internal diameter - 180.0 mm
Brake drum internal diameter after resurfacing -
181.0 mm
minimum brake shoe thickness - 1.0 mm
Torque wrench setting:
Glow plugs - 2,5 m.daN (18 lbf.ft.)
Wheel bolts - 85 Nm

Bulb types:
Headlights:
Non GTI - 45/40W
GTI - H4 (55W)
Front parking - 5W
Indicators - 21W
Front driving (GTI) - H3 (55W)
Stop light - 5/21W
Reverse - 21W
Rear fog - 21W
Interior bulb - 5W

CAPACITIES:

	Litres	Pints
Engine oil including oil filter:		
954 and 1124	4.5	8.0
1360	5.0	8.8
Diesel	5.0	8.8
Cooling system (inc. heater):		
XU5J	6.6	11.6
XV8 and XW7	6.0	10.6
XY7 and XY8	5.8	10.2
Diesel	8.3	14.6
Transmission (manual):		
Petrol	2.0	3.5
Diesel	2.0	3.5
Transmission (automatic):		
Petrol	2.4	

Tyre pressures:

	bar	lb.sq in.
normal:		
145 SRVAN		
front	1.9	28
rear	2.3	33
165/70 SR13 (Automatic)		
front	2.0	29
rear	2.1	30
185/60 HR 14 (CTI)		
front	2.0	29
rear	2.1	30
185/55 VR 15 (GTI)		
front	2.0	29
rear	2.0	29

Wheel alignment or tracking:
Toe-in:
Non GTI - 2.5 mm to 4.5 mm
GTI - 1.0 mm to 3.0 mm

Fuel tank:
50.0 litres - 11.0 gallons

CHAPTER 9 - TOOLS & EQUIPMENT

Although good tools are not cheap, if you reckon their cost against what you would otherwise spend on professional servicing and repairs, your arithmetic should show you that it doesn't take long to recoup your outlay - and then to start showing a profit!

In fact, there is no need to spend a fortune all at once - most owners who do their own servicing acquire their implements over a long period of time. However, there are some items you simply cannot do without in order to properly carry out the work necessary to keep your car on the road. Therefore, in the following lists, we have concen-

trated on those items which are likely to be valuable aids to maintaining your car in a good state of tune, and to keep it running sweetly and safely and in addition we have featured some of the tools that are 'nice-to-have' rather than 'must have' because as your tool chest grows, there are some tools that help to make servicing just that bit easier and more thorough to carry out.

Two vital points - firstly always buy the best quality tools you can afford. 'Cheap and cheerful' items may look similar to more expensive implements, but

experience shows that they often fail when the going gets tough, and some can even be dangerous. With proper care, good quality tools will last a lifetime, and can be regarded as an investment. The extra outlay is well worth it, in the long run.

Over the years, there have been various nut/bolt/spanner designa-tions. For many years British cars standardised on 'AF', a designation referring to the measurement 'across the flats' of the hexagon nut or bolt head, while the 'foreigners' were 'Metric'. While there are still many 'AF' cars around, all modern cars are 'Metric' of course, apart from American cars. (For the record, 'metric' sizes are also measured across their flats!). Be sure you know which designation applies to your car before you start buying. Your local motor accessory store should be able to advise, or you could all your local main dealer to make sure, if necessary.

SPANNERS:

A. The two common types of spanner are the ring and the open-ended. The ring spanner grips practically all round the bolt, and is preferable where the bolt is really tight, for an open-ended spanner, merely strad-dling two flats of the bolt, could slip. On the other hand, the open-end is often quicker and easier to use - so this set of 'Combination' spanners, a ring at one end, open-ended the other, is a nice compromise!

All the tools featured here are available from your local High Street auto-accessory store or Super Store. Any special tools needed for your car are referred to in Chapter 3.

B. While the 'flatness' of the combination spanners (or of a conventional open-ended spanner) is often useful, there are occasions when only the offset, or 'swan neck' of the conventional ring spanner will do the job - like when having to operate over the top of one bolt in order to undo another.

Unlike the combination spanners, the conventional ring and open-ended spanners will have a different size at each end.
Usually, the AF sizes will rise in sixteenths of an inch, and the metrics by one millimetre - the following sizes will probably cover most of your needs:
AF - 3/8 x 7/16, 1/2 x 9/16, 5/8 x 11/16, 13/16 x 7/8
Metric - 10 x 11, 12 x 13, 14 x 15, 16 x 17

C. The sturdy specialist brake spanner used, for brake adjusters or bleed nipples, is undeniably a wise buy, as mentioned in the brake servicing text. You might not need the set as shown here, but you can choose individual sizes to suit your car, such as 1/4 in. square x 11/32 in. square or 1/4 in. hexagonal x 5/16 in. AF, or perhaps 8 x 10mm hexagonal - there are others.

D. A basic socket set should figure highly on your shopping list, for it will cover your basic spanner sizes and can often solve difficult access or extra-leverage problems. This one is a fairly sophisticated set, and includes a number of useful extras, such as spark plug spanners and Allen key and screwdriver bits. Don't buy more than you need, however, and don't be tempted by cheap, nasty - and often dangerous - market stall socket sets.

E. A torque wrench was also once a luxury, but nowadays it's practically essential, with specific torque settings quoted for many of the nuts and bolts used in modern car engineering. The example shown will cater for most applications, including adjustable wheel-bearing hub nuts, but even the next size up (30-150 lb/ft) in the DIY range will still fall short of the 200-odd lb/ft specified for some hub nuts!

F. If you still need a plug spanner, and particularly if your engine features deep-set spark plugs, this Sykes-Pickavant 'extra long plug wrench', combining both 10mm and 14mm sizes, could be a boon. Some plugs are set deeper than the average length of a socket-set spark plug spanner, and if the socket set's extension bar is prone to leaving the spanner socket stuck on the plug, then you could have a problem ...

SCREWDRIVERS:

G. You will need a selection of screwdrivers, both flat-bladed and cross-headed, long ones, short ones, slim ones, fat ones ...

PLIERS:

H. Ordinary combination (or 'engineers') pliers are needed for general work, while a long-nosed pair are handy where access is tight. Their cutting edges are useful for stripping cable insulation, or for snipping wire or trimming split-pin lengths, but you might prefer a pair of specialist side-cutter pliers for such work.

I. Jolly useful as an extra pair of hands, or for gripping such as a rusty nut or bolt really tightly, is a self-grip wrench. This is a long-nose example, but there are also ordinary straight-jaw and round jaw versions.

SUNDRIES:

J. You'll need hammers, including the useful 1lb ball-pein type, plus a hefty copper hammer and maybe a soft (plastic-headed) hammer, too.

K. The wire brush should have brass bristles and as well as an ordinary set of feeler gauges, an 'ignition set' covers most plug and points gap sizes, and includes a points file and a spark plug gap setting tool.

L. You may need a grease gun (although virtually no modern cars have grease points) but you *will* want an oil can, and an oil funnel, and a container of sufficient capacity into which the engine oil can be drained.

M. You may also need a drain plug 'key' suitable for your car unless all the drain plugs are 'bolt'-type hexagons.

N. Well worthwhile, since some oil filters can be cussedly tight, is some sort of oil filter wrench - this chain-type is a nice example. In extreme cases, even these wrenches can fail to get a grip, in which case, drive an old screwdriver right through the filter and twist it loose.

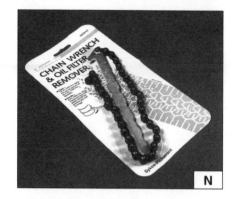

N

O. A separate set of hand-held Allen keys is a good idea (they come in metric or Imperial sizes), and an adjustable spanner and a 'Junior' hacksaw will have their uses.

P. For your weekly maintenance checks, you'll need a tyre pressure gauge, tyre tread depth gauge and a footpump - which might, like the example here, have an integral pressure gauge. And whether you're wheel-changing at home or roadside, you will welcome the extremely useful Sykes-Pickavant 'Wheelmaster' wrench, which can be extended to give enough leverage to shift those wheel nuts or bolts that the average car-kit wheelbrace wouldn't even look at - see the wheel-change routine at the start of Chapter 3. Remember to carry the extendable wrench with you in the car!

O

LIFTING:

Q. While the jack supplied with the car *might* be OK for emergency wheel-changes, you would soon tire of trying to use it for servicing operations. Here, you need a good trolley jack, and one of the latest on the market is this 2-ton lifting capacity 'Lift and Lock' example which, as its name suggests, has a built-in fail-safe locking device in the event of hydraulic failure.

R. No matter what sort of jack you use, it is ESSENTIAL that you should not venture beneath a car supported on a jack alone. Having raised it, you need to support it safely and securely. What you need now is definitely NOT house bricks (or any other such potentially dangerous items!) but rather axle stands or wheel-ramps. Adjustable-height stands are essential and both axle stands and ramps should be produced by a 'name' manufacturer, for safety's sake. If you don't need the wheels off, it can be argued that the ramps offer better stability - though you'll benefit from some assistance when it comes to driving upon them. See the start of *Chapter 3*.

P

TUNING AIDS:

S. As we have said earlier in this chapter and within the servicing sections, the tuning aids that are now available to the DIY market have become practically invaluable 'musts' for the dedicated home mechanic. Any of the Gunson's collection shown here would soon prove their worth. Top of the tree, of course, is their 'Gastester Professional' - don't let its designation suggest that it's not for DIY use, for although it's expensive a group of friends sharing its cost would find their outlay well worth the benefits offered by the unit's Exhaust Gas 'CO' functions, plus its Voltage, Dwell and RPM modes. If it's pure 'multi-meter' you're after, then their 'Digimeter 320' is a tidy little hand-held unit, with clear digital read-outs for such as Volts (DC and household AC) and Amps, Ohms, rpm, and Dwell (degrees and per cent), and its sophistication

Q

extends to Frequency, Period and Pulsewidth testing (handy for fuel injection systems), as well as Diode, Resistance and Continuity testing. Also by Gunson's is the powerful 'Timestrobe' xenon timing light, the now not so new, but still novel 'Colortune' and (not shown) the 'Carbalancer'. The latter two devices are virtually invaluable when it comes to carburettor tuning.

R

S

APPENDIX 1
RECOMMENDED LUBRICANTS
& ESSENTIAL FLUIDS

Castrol has a broad range of top-quality oils, greases and other essential fluids, and they will all figure in the 'Recommended' list appended to the handbooks issued by the major motor manufacturers.

POWER STEERING
Castrol Dexron R III

BRAKE FLUID
Castrol Universal Brake Fluid

WHEEL BEARINGS
Castrol LM grease

ENGINE OIL

PETROL ENGINES
GTX (15W/50): The 'superior' multigrade engine oil that is certainly suitable for newer vehicles requiring an SAE 15W/50 or 20W/50 viscosity oil, but which is particularly appropriate for older technology engines and high-mileage vehicles, where working clearances might be higher than average.

GTX Protection Plus (15W/40): Suits newer vehicles, including turbo-charged, where this viscosity is recommended. Very low phospherous content to prolong catalyst life.

GTX Magnatec (10W/40): "The unique molecular attraction protects your engine from the moment you turn your key, providing complete, continuous protection at all times", say Castrol.

DIESEL ENGINES
GTD (15W/40): Specially formulated for the particular demands of all diesel engines, including turbo-charged.

GEARBOX OIL

MANUAL TRANSMISSION
Castrol Syntrax Universal

AUTOMATIC TRANSMISSION
Castrol Dexron R III

LOCKS AND HINGES
Castrol Everyman

ELECTRICAL CONNECTIONS
Castrol DWF

NUT AND BOLT RELEASE
Castrol Easing Oil

COOLING SYSTEM
Castrol Antifreeze & Summer Coolant

CASTROL ANTI-FREEZE: Recommended for use in petrol or diesel engine cooling systems, with aluminium or cast engines. Its formulation of mono ethylene glycol and corrosion inhibitors makes it suitable for all-year-round use, and because it contains no phosphate it is reckoned that the problems of deposits in some modern uprated engines are eliminated. A 33 per cent concentration will protect down to minus 17 degrees C.

APPENDIX 2
SPECIALISTS & SUPPLIERS
FEATURED IN THIS BOOK

All of the products and specialists listed below have contributed in various ways to this book. All of the consumer products used are available through regular high street outlets or by mail order from specialist suppliers.

Castrol (UK) Ltd., Burmah House, Pipers Way, Swindon, Wiltshire, SN3 1RE. Tel: 01793 452222
Contact Castrol's Consumer Technical Department Help Line on the above number for advice on lubrication recommendations.

Dinol (GB) Ltd., Dinol House, 98 Ock Street, Abingdon, Oxford, OX14 5DH. Tel: 01235 530677
Suppliers of Dinitrol rust proofing fluids, and are equipped to carry out rustproofing on vehicles.

Gunson Ltd., Coppen Road, Dagenham, Essex, RM8 1NU. Tel: 0181 984 8855
Electrical and electronic engine tuning equipment.

HPI Autodata, HP Information plc, Dolphin House, P O Box 61, New Street, Salisbury, Wiltshire, SP1 2TB. Tel: 01722 422422
Before buying any used car, check it out with HPI Autodata.

NGK Spark Plugs (UK) Ltd., 7-8-9 Garrick Industrial Centre, Hendon, London, NW9 6AQ. Tel: 0181 202 2151
Top quality spark plugs.

SP Tyres UK Ltd., Fort Dunlop, Birmingham, B24 9QT. Tel: 0121 384 4444
Manufacturers of Dunlop tyres.

Sykes-Pickavant Group plc, Kilnhouse Lane, Lytham St Annes, Lancs, FY8 3DU. Tel: 01253 721291
Wide range of hand tools and specialist equipment, some of which were used in this book.

Signam Limited, Harris Road, Warwick CV34 5FY. Tel: 01926 492685
Signam superlative number plates made to BSAU145a available from Halfords and all good accessory shops.

Waste Oil Disposal
There are 1,300 listed waste oil disposal sites in the UK alone. PLEASE don't foul the environment by tipping waste oil into the drains or the ground. Find your nearest oil disposal point by running the National Rivers Authority on FREEPHONE 0800 663366.

PORTER MANUALS *ON DISK!*
The Service Guides that take you from computer.... to your car!
- **Step-by-step instructions** (120 pages in all) and 50 line drawings to print out and use.
- **Facts & Figures** - service data with computer search for key words and information.
- **Interactive FAULT FINDING program** - solve engine, electrics, find system problems using computerised logic.
- Complete with print-out folder.
- Works on ANY computer running **Windows 3.0, 3.1, 3.11** or **Windows 95**.
- 3½" floppy disk - no CD drive necessary!

Many PORTER MANUALS are also available as DiskMANUALS.
Ask your retailer or please contact Porter Publishing in case of difficulty.

APPENDIX 3
SERVICE HISTORY

This Chapter helps you keep track of all the servicing carried out on your vehicle and can even save you money! A vehicle with a Service History is always worth more than one without, and you can make full use of this section, even if you have a garage or mechanic carry out the work for you. It enables you to specify the jobs you want to have carried out to your vehicle and, of course, it enables you to keep that all-important Service History. And even if your vehicle doesn't have a 'history' going back to when it was new, keeping this Chapter complete will add to your vehicle's value when you come to sell it. Mind you, it obviously won't be enough to just to tick the boxes: keep all your receipts when you buy oil, filters and other consumables or parts. That way, you'll also be able to return any faulty parts if needs be.

Buying Parts

Before carrying out a service on your car, you will need to purchase the right parts. Please refer to **Chapter 2, Buying Guide** for information on how to buy the right parts at the right prices and for information on how to find your car's 'identity numbers'; information that you will need in order to buy the right parts, first time!

The Job Lists

Wherever possible, the Jobs listed in this section have been placed in a logical order or placed into groups that will help you make progress on the car. We have tried to save you too much in the way of unnecessary movement by grouping jobs around areas of the car. Therefore, at each Service Interval, you will see the work grouped into Jobs that need carrying out in The Engine Bay, Around The Car or Under The Car.

You'll also see space at each Service Interval for you to write down the date, price and seller's name every time you buy consumables or accessories. And once again, do remember to keep your receipts! There's also space for you to date and sign the Service Record or for a garage's stamp to be applied.

As you move through the Service Intervals, you will notice that the work carried out at say, **1,500 Miles or Every**

Month, whichever comes first, is repeated at each one of the following Service Intervals. The same applies to the **6,000 Miles or Six Months** interval: much of it is repeated at **12,000 Miles or Twelve Months.** Every time a Job or set of Jobs is 'repeated' from an earlier Interval, we show it in a tinted area on the page. You can then see more clearly which jobs are unique to the level of Service Interval that you are on.

You will also find that all the major Intervals, right up to the 'longest', contain Jobs that are unique to that Service Interval. That's why we have continued this Service History right up to the **36,000 Miles or every Three Years** interval. So now, you will be able to service your car and keep a full record of the work, in the knowledge that your car has been looked after as well as anyone could wish for!

Important Note!

The Service Jobs listed here are intended as a check list and a means of keeping a record of your vehicle's service history, **not** as a set of instructions for working on your car. It is most important that you refer to **Chapter 3, Servicing Your Car** for full details of how to carry out each Job listed here and for essential SAFETY information and, see also, **Chapter 1, Safety First!**.

EVERY 500 MILES, WEEKLY OR BEFORE A LONG JOURNEY

This list is shown, complete, only once. It would have been a bit much to have provided the list 52 times over for use once a week throughout the year! Each job is, however, included with every longer Service list from 3,000 miles/Three Months-on so that each of the 'weekly' Jobs is carried out as part of every service.

Every 500 Miles - The Engine Bay

☐ Job 1. Engine oil level.

☐ Job 2. Check coolant level.

☐ Job 3. Brake fluid level.

☐ Job 4. Check windscreen wash level.

Every 500 Miles - Around the Car

☐ Job 5. Check tyre pressures.

☐ Job 6. Check front lights and indicators.

☐ Job 7. Check side indicator repeaters.

☐ Job 8. Check rear lights.

☐ Job 9. Number plate lights.

☐ Job 10. Interior lights.

☐ Job 11. Check windscreen wipers.

☐ Job 12. Windscreen washers.

EVERY 1,500 MILES - OR EVERY MONTH, WHICHEVER COMES FIRST

These Jobs are similar to the 500 Mile Jobs but don't need carrying out quite so regularly. Once again, these Jobs are not shown with a separate listing for each 1,500 miles/1 Month interval but they are included as part of every 3,000 miles/Three Months Service list and for every longer Service interval.

Every 1,500 Miles - Around the Car

☐ Job 13. Check battery electrolyte level.

☐ Job 14. Check horn.

Every 1,500 Miles - Under the Car

☐ Job 15. Check tyre treads.

☐ Job 16. Check spare wheel.

☐ Job 17. Touch-up paintwork.

☐ Job 18. Valet interior.

☐ Job 19. Improve visibility.

EVERY 3,000 MILES - OR THREE MONTHS, WHICHEVER COMES FIRST

All the Service Jobs in the tinted area have been carried forward from earlier service intervals and are to be repeated at this service.

Every 3,000 Miles - The Engine Bay

First carry out all Jobs listed under earlier Service intervals as applicable.

☐ Job 1. Engine oil level.

☐ Job 2. Check coolant level.

☐ Job 3. Brake fluid level.

☐ Job 4. Check windscreen wash level.

☐ Job 20. Check alternator drive belt.

☐ Job 21. **DIESEL ENGINED MODELS ONLY** Check vacuum pump drive belt.

☐ Job 22. **DIESEL ENGINES ONLY** Drain fuel filter.

☐ Job 23. **DIESEL ENGINES ONLY** Renew diesel engine oil.

☐ Job 24. Replace diesel engine oil filter.

☐ Job 25. Check brake and fuel lines.

☐ Job 26. Check air filter.

Every 3,000 Miles - Around The Car

First carry out all Jobs listed under earlier Service intervals as applicable.

☐ Job 5. Check tyre pressures.

☐ Job 6. Check front lights and indicators.

☐ Job 7. Check side indicator repeaters.

☐ Job 8. Check rear lights.

☐ Job 9. Number plate lights.

☐ Job 10. Interior lights.

☐ Job 11. Check windscreen wipers.

☐ Job 12. Windscreen washers.

☐ Job 13. Check battery electrolyte level.

☐ Job 14. Check horn.

☐ Job 27. Check wheel bolts.

☐ Job 28. Check handbrake adjustment.

☐ Job 29. Check ABS warning light.

☐ Job 30. Check windscreen.

☐ Job 31. Check and lubricate aerial.

Every 3,000 Miles - Under the Car

First carry out all Jobs listed under earlier Service intervals as applicable.

☐ Job 15. Check tyre treads.

☐ Job 16. Check spare wheel.

☐ Job 17. Touch-up paintwork.

☐ Job 18. Valet interior.

☐ Job 19. Improve visibility.

☐ Job 32. Check exhaust system and mountings.

☐ Job 33. Check brake and fuel lines.

☐ Job 34. Check steering rack gaiters.

☐ Job 35. Check drive shaft gaiters.

☐ Job 36. Check underside of car for leaks.

☐ Job 37. Clean mud traps.

Every 3,000 Miles - Road Test

☐ Job 38. Clean controls.

☐ Job 39. Check instruments and controls.

☐ Job 40. Check throttle action.

☐ Job 41. Check clutch action.

☐ Job 42. Road test: brakes and steering.

☐ Job 43. Check C.V. joints for noise.

☐ Job 44. Check automatic transmission fluid.

Date serviced:...

Carried out by: ....
Garage Stamp or signature:

Parts/Accessories purchased (date, parts,

source) ....

....

....

....

....

EVERY 6,000 MILES - OR EVERY SIX MONTHS, WHICHEVER COMES FIRST

All the Service Jobs in the tinted area have been carried forward from earlier service intervals and are to be repeated at this service.

Every 6,000 Miles - The Engine Bay

First carry out all Jobs listed under earlier Service intervals as applicable.

☐ Job 2. Check coolant level.

☐ Job 3. Brake fluid level.

☐ Job 4. Check windscreen wash level.

☐ Job 20. Check alternator drive belt.

☐ Job 21. **DIESEL ENGINED MODELS ONLY** Check vacuum pump drive belt.

☐ Job 22. **DIESEL ENGINES ONLY** Drain fuel filter.

☐ Job 23. **DIESEL ENGINES ONLY** Renew diesel engine oil.

☐ Job 24. Replace diesel engine oil filter.

☐ Job 25. Check brake and fuel lines.

☐ Job 45. Change engine oil and filter.

☐ Job 46. Clean and check spark plugs.

☐ Job 47. Clean and check ignition components.

☐ Job 48. Check water pump.

☐ Job 49. Lubricate/adjust clutch cable.

☐ Job 50. Check gearbox oil level.

☐ Job 51. Check power steering fluid level (where fitted).

☐ Job 52. Check and turn air cleaner element.

☐ Job 53. Lubricate throttle linkage.

☐ Job 54. Lubricate carburettor/diesel pump linkages.

☐ Job 55. Adjust carburettor.

☐ Job 56. Check idle speed and mixture.

☐ Job 57. Check exhaust emission.

☐ Job 58. Check pipes and hoses.

☐ Job 59. Lubricate bonnet release.

Every 6,000 Miles - Around the Car

First carry out all Jobs listed under earlier Service intervals as applicable.

- [ ] Job 5. Check tyre pressures.
- [ ] Job 6. Check front lights and indicators.
- [ ] Job 7. Check side indicator repeaters.
- [ ] Job 8. Check rear lights.
- [ ] Job 9. Number plate lights.
- [ ] Job 10. Interior lights.
- [ ] Job 11. Check windscreen wipers.
- [ ] Job 12. Windscreen washers.
- [ ] Job 13. Check battery electrolyte level.
- [ ] Job 14. Check horn.
- [ ] Job 27. Check wheel bolts.
- [ ] Job 28. Check handbrake adjustment.
- [ ] Job 29. Check ABS warning light.
- [ ] Job 30. Check windscreen.
- [ ] Job 31. Check and lubricate aerial.

- [ ] Job 60. Check seat belts and mountings.
- [ ] Job 61. Check seat mountings.
- [ ] Job 62. Check fuel filler-cap seal.
- [ ] Job 63. Lubricate hinges, locks, check straps.
- [ ] Job 64. Check shock absorber action.
- [ ] Job 65. Check wheel alignment.

Every 6,000 Miles - Under the Car

First carry out all Jobs listed under earlier Service intervals as applicable.

- [ ] Job 15. Check tyre treads.
- [ ] Job 16. Check spare wheel.
- [ ] Job 17. Touch-up paintwork.
- [ ] Job 18. Valet interior.
- [ ] Job 19. Improve visibility.
- [ ] Job 32. Check exhaust system and mountings.
- [ ] Job 33. Check brake and fuel lines.
- [ ] Job 34. Check steering rack gaiters.
- [ ] Job 35. Check drive shaft gaiters.
- [ ] Job 36. Check underside of car for leaks.
- [ ] Job 37. Clean mud traps.

- [ ] Job 66. Check/renew front brake pads.
- [ ] Job 67. Check brake discs.
- [ ] Job 68. Check rear brake shoes.
- [ ] Job 69. Check/renew rear brake pads.
- [ ] Job 70. Check rear brake discs.
- [ ] Job 71. Check brake proportioning valve.
- [ ] Job 72. Check steering ball-joints.

Every 6,000 Miles - Road Test

- [ ] Job 38. Clean controls.
- [ ] Job 39. Check instruments and controls.
- [ ] Job 40. Check throttle action.
- [ ] Job 41. Check clutch action.
- [ ] Job 42. Road test: brakes and steering.
- [ ] Job 43. Check C.V. joints for noise.
- [ ] Job 44. Check automatic transmission fluid.

EVERY 9,000 MILES - OR EVERY NINE MONTHS, WHICHEVER COMES FIRST

All the Jobs at this Service Interval have been carried forward from earlier Service Intervals and are to be repeated at this service.

Every 9,000 Miles - The Engine Bay

- [ ] Job 1. Engine oil level.
- [ ] Job 2. Check coolant level.
- [ ] Job 3. Brake fluid level.
- [ ] Job 4. Check windscreen wash level.
- [ ] Job 20. Check alternator drive belt.
- [ ] Job 21. **DIESEL ENGINED MODELS ONLY** Check vacuum pump drive belt.
- [ ] Job 22. **DIESEL ENGINES ONLY** Drain fuel filter.
- [ ] Job 23. **DIESEL ENGINES ONLY** Renew diesel engine oil.
- [ ] Job 24. Replace diesel engine oil filter.
- [ ] Job 25. Check brake and fuel lines.
- [ ] Job 26. Check air filter.

Date serviced:...

Carried out by: ....
Garage Stamp or signature:

Parts/Accessories purchased (date, parts, source) ....
....
....
....
....

Every 9,000 Miles - Around The Car

First carry out all Jobs listed under earlier Service intervals as applicable.

- [ ] Job 5. Check tyre pressures.
- [ ] Job 6. Check front lights and indicators.
- [ ] Job 7. Check side indicator repeaters.
- [ ] Job 8. Check rear lights.
- [ ] Job 9. Number plate lights.
- [ ] Job 10. Interior lights.
- [ ] Job 11. Check windscreen wipers.
- [ ] Job 12. Windscreen washers.
- [ ] Job 13. Check battery electrolyte level.
- [ ] Job 14. Check horn.
- [ ] Job 27. Check wheel bolts.
- [ ] Job 28. Check handbrake adjustment.
- [ ] Job 29. Check ABS warning light.
- [ ] Job 30. Check windscreen.
- [ ] Job 31. Check and lubricate aerial.

Every 9,000 Miles - Under the Car

First carry out all Jobs listed under earlier Service intervals as applicable.

- [ ] Job 15. Check tyre treads.
- [ ] Job 16. Check spare wheel.
- [ ] Job 17. Touch-up paintwork.
- [ ] Job 18. Valet interior.
- [ ] Job 19. Improve visibility.
- [ ] Job 32. Check exhaust system and mountings.
- [ ] Job 33. Check brake and fuel lines.
- [ ] Job 34. Check steering rack gaiters.
- [ ] Job 35. Check drive shaft gaiters.
- [ ] Job 36. Check underside of car for leaks.
- [ ] Job 37. Clean mud traps.

Every 9,000 Miles - Road Test

- [ ] Job 38. Clean controls.
- [ ] Job 39. Check instruments and controls.
- [ ] Job 40. Check throttle action.
- [ ] Job 41. Check clutch action.
- [ ] Job 42. Road test: brakes and steering.
- [ ] Job 43. Check C.V. joints for noise.
- [ ] Job 44. Check automatic transmission fluid.

Date serviced:..

Carried out by: ....
Garage Stamp or signature:

Parts/Accessories purchased (date, parts, source) ....
....
....
....
....

EVERY 12,000 MILES - OR EVERY TWELVE MONTHS, WHICHEVER COMES FIRST

All the Service Jobs in the tinted area have been carried forward from earlier service intervals and are to be repeated at this service.

Every 12,000 Miles - The Engine Bay

First carry out all Jobs listed under earlier Service intervals as applicable.

- [ ] Job 4. Check windscreen wash level.
- [ ] Job 20. Check alternator drive belt.
- [ ] Job 21. DIESEL ENGINED MODELS ONLY Check vacuum pump drive belt.
- [ ] Job 22. DIESEL ENGINES ONLY Drain fuel filter.
- [ ] Job 23. DIESEL ENGINES ONLY Renew diesel engine oil.
- [ ] Job 24. Replace diesel engine oil filter.
- [ ] Job 25. Check brake and fuel lines.
- [ ] Job 45. Change engine oil and filter.
- [ ] Job 47. Clean and check ignition components.
- [ ] Job 48. Check water pump.
- [ ] Job 49. Lubricate/adjust clutch cable.
- [ ] Job 50. Check gearbox oil level.
- [ ] Job 51. Check power steering fluid level (where fitted).
- [ ] Job 52. Check and turn air cleaner element.
- [ ] Job 53. Lubricate throttle linkage.
- [ ] Job 54. Lubricate carburettor/diesel pump linkages.
- [ ] Job 55. Adjust carburettor.
- [ ] Job 56. Check idle speed and mixture.
- [ ] Job 57. Check exhaust emission.
- [ ] Job 58. Check pipes and hoses.
- [ ] Job 59. Lubricate bonnet release.

- [ ] Job 73. Change air cleaner element and clean housing.
- [ ] Job 74. Check and adjust valve clearances.
- [ ] Job 75. NOT DIESEL, OR PETROL MODELS WITH CATALYST Check ignition timing.

SERVICE HISTORY

- [ ] Job 76. Check coolant.
- [ ] Job 77. Check vacuum hoses.
- [ ] Job 78. Check/renew crankcase emission hoses.
- [ ] Job 79. Clean oil filler cap.
- [ ] Job 80. **DIESEL ENGINES ONLY** Check air-pump belt.
- [ ] Job 81. Renew spark plugs.
- [ ] Job 82. **DIESEL ENGINES ONLY** Clean glow plugs.
- [ ] Job 83. Clean/protect battery terminals.
- [ ] Job 84. Check battery specific gravity.
- [ ] Job 85. Replace fuel filter.
- [ ] Job 86. Fault code readout.
- [ ] Job 87. Check tool kit and jack.
- [ ] Job 88. Check light unit seals.
- [ ] Job 89. Check door/tailgate seals.
- [ ] Job 90. Adjust headlight alignment.
- [ ] Job 91. Renew wiper blades.
- [ ] Job 92. Check soft-top and frame.
- [ ] Job 93. Check floors.
- [ ] Job 94. Renew batteries in car alarm sender.
- [ ] Job 95. Check wiring and terminals.
- [ ] Job 96. Clean radiator exterior.

Every 12,000 Miles - Around the Car

- [ ] Job 5. Check tyre pressures.
- [ ] Job 6. Check front lights and indicators.
- [ ] Job 7. Check side indicator repeaters.
- [ ] Job 8. Check rear lights.
- [ ] Job 9. Number plate lights.
- [ ] Job 10. Interior lights.
- [ ] Job 11. Check windscreen wipers.
- [ ] Job 12. Windscreen washers.
- [ ] Job 13. Check battery electrolyte level.
- [ ] Job 14. Check horn.
- [ ] Job 27. Check wheel bolts.
- [ ] Job 29. Check ABS warning light.
- [ ] Job 30. Check windscreen.
- [ ] Job 31. Check and lubricate aerial.

- [ ] Job 60. Check seat belts and mountings.
- [ ] Job 61. Check seat mountings.
- [ ] Job 62. Check fuel filler-cap seal.
- [ ] Job 63. Lubricate hinges, locks, check straps.
- [ ] Job 64. Check shock absorber action.
- [ ] Job 65. Check wheel alignment.

Every 12,000 Miles - Under the Car

First carry out all Jobs listed under earlier Service intervals as applicable.

- [ ] Job 15. Check tyre treads.
- [ ] Job 16. Check spare wheel.
- [ ] Job 17. Touch-up paintwork.
- [ ] Job 18. Valet interior.
- [ ] Job 19. Improve visibility.
- [ ] Job 32. Check exhaust system and mountings.
- [ ] Job 33. Check brake and fuel lines.
- [ ] Job 34. Check steering rack gaiters.
- [ ] Job 35. Check drive shaft gaiters.
- [ ] Job 36. Check underside of car for leaks.
- [ ] Job 37. Clean mud traps.
- [ ] Job 66. Check/renew front brake pads.
- [ ] Job 67. Check brake discs.
- [ ] Job 68. Check rear brake shoes.
- [ ] Job 69. Check/renew rear brake pads.
- [ ] Job 70. Check rear brake discs.
- [ ] Job 71. Check brake proportioning valve.
- [ ] Job 72. Check steering ball-joints.

- [ ] Job 97. Check wheel bearings.
- [ ] Job 98. Check steering and suspension.
- [ ] Job 99. Check steering rack mountings.
- [ ] Job 100. Check front suspension units.
- [ ] Job 101. Check front suspension bushes.
- [ ] Job 102. Check rear springs and shock absorbers.
- [ ] Job 103. Check rear suspension bushes.
- [ ] Job 104. Check engine and gearbox mountings.

- [ ] Job 105. Check/adjust/lubricate handbrake cable.
- [ ] Job 106. Check underside of body structure.
- [ ] Job 107. Clear drainage holes.
- [ ] Job 108. Renew brake fluid.

Every 12,000 Miles - Road Test

- [ ] Job 38. Clean controls.
- [ ] Job 39. Check instruments and controls.
- [ ] Job 40. Check throttle action.
- [ ] Job 41. Check clutch action.
- [ ] Job 42. Road test: brakes and steering.
- [ ] Job 43. Check C.V. joints for noise.
- [ ] Job 44. Check automatic transmission fluid.

Date serviced:..

Carried out by: ....
Garage Stamp or signature:

Parts/Accessories purchased (date, parts, source) ....
....
....
....
....

EVERY 15,000 MILES - OR EVERY FIFTEEN MONTHS, WHICHEVER COMES FIRST

All the Jobs at this Service Interval have been carried forward from earlier Service Intervals and are to be repeated at this service.

Every 15,000 Miles - The Engine Bay

- [ ] Job 1. Engine oil level.
- [ ] Job 2. Check coolant level.
- [ ] Job 3. Brake fluid level.
- [ ] Job 4. Check windscreen wash level.
- [ ] Job 20. Check alternator drive belt.
- [ ] Job 21. **DIESEL ENGINED MODELS ONLY** Check vacuum pump drive belt.
- [ ] Job 22. **DIESEL ENGINES ONLY** Drain fuel filter.
- [ ] Job 23. **DIESEL ENGINES ONLY** Renew diesel engine oil.
- [ ] Job 24. Replace diesel engine oil filter.
- [ ] Job 25. Check brake and fuel lines.
- [ ] Job 26. Check air filter.

Every 15,000 Miles - Around The Car

First carry out all Jobs listed under earlier Service intervals as applicable.

- [ ] Job 5. Check tyre pressures.
- [ ] Job 6. Check front lights and indicators.
- [ ] Job 7. Check side indicator repeaters.
- [ ] Job 8. Check rear lights.
- [ ] Job 9. Number plate lights.
- [ ] Job 10. Interior lights.
- [ ] Job 11. Check windscreen wipers.
- [ ] Job 12. Windscreen washers.
- [ ] Job 13. Check battery electrolyte level.
- [ ] Job 14. Check horn.
- [ ] Job 27. Check wheel bolts.
- [ ] Job 28. Check handbrake adjustment.
- [ ] Job 29. Check ABS warning light.
- [ ] Job 30. Check windscreen.
- [ ] Job 31. Check and lubricate aerial.

Every 15,000 Miles - Under the Car

First carry out all Jobs listed under earlier Service intervals as applicable.

- [ ] Job 15. Check tyre treads.
- [ ] Job 16. Check spare wheel.
- [ ] Job 17. Touch-up paintwork.
- [ ] Job 18. Valet interior.
- [ ] Job 19. Improve visibility.
- [ ] Job 32. Check exhaust system and mountings.
- [ ] Job 33. Check brake and fuel lines.
- [ ] Job 34. Check steering rack gaiters.
- [ ] Job 35. Check drive shaft gaiters.
- [ ] Job 36. Check underside of car for leaks.
- [ ] Job 37. Clean mud traps.

Every 15,000 Miles - Road Test

- [ ] Job 38. Clean controls.
- [ ] Job 39. Check instruments and controls.
- [ ] Job 40. Check throttle action.
- [ ] Job 41. Check clutch action.
- [ ] Job 42. Road test: brakes and steering.
- [ ] Job 43. Check C.V. joints for noise.
- [ ] Job 44. Check automatic transmission fluid.

Date serviced:..

Carried out by: ....
Garage Stamp or signature:

Parts/Accessories purchased (date, parts, source) ....

....

....

....

....

EVERY 18,000 MILES - OR EVERY EIGHTEEN MONTHS, WHICHEVER COMES FIRST

All the Jobs at this Service Interval have been carried forward from earlier Service Intervals and are to be repeated at this service.

Every 18,000 Miles - The Engine Bay

- [ ] Job 2. Check coolant level.
- [ ] Job 3. Brake fluid level.
- [ ] Job 4. Check windscreen wash level.
- [ ] Job 20. Check alternator drive belt.
- [ ] Job 21. DIESEL ENGINED MODELS ONLY Check vacuum pump drive belt.
- [ ] Job 22. DIESEL ENGINES ONLY Drain fuel filter.
- [ ] Job 23. DIESEL ENGINES ONLY Renew diesel engine oil.
- [ ] Job 24. Replace diesel engine oil filter.
- [ ] Job 25. Check brake and fuel lines.
- [ ] Job 45. Change engine oil and filter.
- [ ] Job 46. Clean and check spark plugs.
- [ ] Job 47. Clean and check ignition components.
- [ ] Job 48. Check water pump.
- [ ] Job 49. Lubricate/adjust clutch cable.
- [ ] Job 50. Check gearbox oil level.
- [ ] Job 51. Check power steering fluid level (where fitted).
- [ ] Job 52. Check and turn air cleaner element.
- [ ] Job 53. Lubricate throttle linkage.
- [ ] Job 54. Lubricate carburettor/diesel pump linkages.
- [ ] Job 55. Adjust carburettor.
- [ ] Job 56. Check idle speed and mixture.
- [ ] Job 57. Check exhaust emission.
- [ ] Job 58. Check pipes and hoses.
- [ ] Job 59. Lubricate bonnet release.

Every 18,000 Miles - Around the Car

- [ ] Job 5. Check tyre pressures.
- [ ] Job 6. Check front lights and indicators.
- [ ] Job 7. Check side indicator repeaters.
- [ ] Job 8. Check rear lights.
- [ ] Job 9. Number plate lights.
- [ ] Job 10. Interior lights.
- [ ] Job 11. Check windscreen wipers.
- [ ] Job 12. Windscreen washers.
- [ ] Job 13. Check battery electrolyte level.
- [ ] Job 14. Check horn.
- [ ] Job 27. Check wheel bolts.
- [ ] Job 29. Check ABS warning light.
- [ ] Job 30. Check windscreen.
- [ ] Job 31. Check and lubricate aerial.
- [ ] Job 60. Check seat belts and mountings.
- [ ] Job 61. Check seat mountings.
- [ ] Job 62. Check fuel filler-cap seal.
- [ ] Job 63. Lubricate hinges, locks, check straps.
- [ ] Job 64. Check shock absorber action.
- [ ] Job 65. Check wheel alignment.

Every 18,000 Miles - Under the Car

First carry out all Jobs listed under earlier Service intervals as applicable.

- [ ] Job 15. Check tyre treads.
- [ ] Job 16. Check spare wheel.
- [ ] Job 17. Touch-up paintwork.
- [ ] Job 18. Valet interior.
- [ ] Job 19. Improve visibility.
- [ ] Job 32. Check exhaust system and mountings.
- [ ] Job 33. Check brake and fuel lines.
- [ ] Job 34. Check steering rack gaiters.
- [ ] Job 35. Check drive shaft gaiters.
- [ ] Job 36. Check underside of car for leaks.
- [ ] Job 37. Clean mud traps.
- [ ] Job 66. Check/renew front brake pads.
- [ ] Job 67. Check brake discs.
- [ ] Job 68. Check rear brake shoes.
- [ ] Job 69. Check/renew rear brake pads.
- [ ] Job 70. Check rear brake discs.
- [ ] Job 71. Check brake proportioning valve.
- [ ] Job 72. Check steering ball-joints.

Every 18,000 Miles - Road Test

- [ ] Job 38. Clean controls.
- [ ] Job 39. Check instruments and controls.
- [ ] Job 40. Check throttle action.
- [ ] Job 41. Check clutch action.
- [ ] Job 42. Road test: brakes and steering.
- [ ] Job 43. Check C.V. joints for noise.
- [ ] Job 44. Check automatic transmission fluid.

Date serviced:..

Carried out by:..
Garage Stamp or signature:

Parts/Accessories purchased (date, parts, source) ....
....
....
....
....

EVERY 21,000 MILES - OR EVERY TWENTY ONE MONTHS, WHICHEVER COMES FIRST

All the Jobs at this Service Interval have been carried forward from earlier Service Intervals and are to be repeated at this service.

Every 21,000 Miles - The Engine Bay

- [ ] Job 1. Engine oil level.
- [ ] Job 2. Check coolant level.
- [ ] Job 3. Brake fluid level.
- [ ] Job 4. Check windscreen wash level.
- [ ] Job 20. Check alternator drive belt.
- [ ] Job 21. **DIESEL ENGINED MODELS ONLY** Check vacuum pump drive belt.
- [ ] Job 22. **DIESEL ENGINES ONLY** Drain fuel filter.
- [ ] Job 23. **DIESEL ENGINES ONLY** Renew diesel engine oil.
- [ ] Job 24. Replace diesel engine oil filter.
- [ ] Job 25. Check brake and fuel lines.
- [ ] Job 26. Check air filter.

Every 21,000 Miles - Around the Car

First carry out all Jobs listed under earlier Service intervals as applicable.

- [ ] Job 5. Check tyre pressures.
- [ ] Job 6. Check front lights and indicators.
- [ ] Job 7. Check side indicator repeaters.
- [ ] Job 8. Check rear lights.
- [ ] Job 9. Number plate lights.
- [ ] Job 10. Interior lights.
- [ ] Job 11. Check windscreen wipers.
- [ ] Job 12. Windscreen washers.
- [ ] Job 13. Check battery electrolyte level.
- [ ] Job 14. Check horn.
- [ ] Job 27. Check wheel bolts.
- [ ] Job 28. Check handbrake adjustment.
- [ ] Job 29. Check ABS warning light.
- [ ] Job 30. Check windscreen.
- [ ] Job 31. Check and lubricate aerial.

Every 21,000 Miles - Under the Car

First carry out all Jobs listed under earlier Service intervals as applicable.

- [ ] Job 15. Check tyre treads.
- [ ] Job 16. Check spare wheel.
- [ ] Job 17. Touch-up paintwork.
- [ ] Job 18. Valet interior.
- [ ] Job 19. Improve visibility.
- [ ] Job 32. Check exhaust system and mountings.
- [ ] Job 33. Check brake and fuel lines.
- [ ] Job 34. Check steering rack gaiters.
- [ ] Job 35. Check drive shaft gaiters.
- [ ] Job 36. Check underside of car for leaks.
- [ ] Job 37. Clean mud traps.

Every 21,000 Miles - Road Test

- [ ] Job 38. Clean controls.
- [ ] Job 39. Check instruments and controls.
- [ ] Job 40. Check throttle action.
- [ ] Job 41. Check clutch action.
- [ ] Job 42. Road test: brakes and steering.
- [ ] Job 43. Check C.V. joints for noise.
- [ ] Job 44. Check automatic transmission fluid.

Date serviced:..

Carried out by: ....
Garage Stamp or signature:

Parts/Accessories purchased (date, parts, source) ....

....

....

....

....

EVERY 24,000 MILES - OR EVERY TWO YEARS, WHICHEVER COMES FIRST

All the Service Jobs in the tinted area have been carried forward from earlier service intervals and are to be repeated at this service.

Every 24,000 Miles - The Engine Bay

First carry out all Jobs listed under earlier Service intervals as applicable.

- [ ] Job 4. Check windscreen wash level.
- [ ] Job 20. Check alternator drive belt.
- [ ] Job 21. DIESEL ENGINED MODELS ONLY Check vacuum pump drive belt.
- [ ] Job 22. DIESEL ENGINES ONLY Drain fuel filter.
- [ ] Job 23. DIESEL ENGINES ONLY Renew diesel engine oil.
- [ ] Job 24. Replace diesel engine oil filter.
- [ ] Job 25. Check brake and fuel lines.
- [ ] Job 45. Change engine oil and filter.
- [ ] Job 47. Clean and check ignition components.
- [ ] Job 48. Check water pump.
- [ ] Job 49. Lubricate/adjust clutch cable.
- [ ] Job 50. Check gearbox oil level.
- [ ] Job 51. Check power steering fluid level (where fitted).
- [ ] Job 52. Check and turn air cleaner element.
- [ ] Job 53. Lubricate throttle linkage.
- [ ] Job 54. Lubricate carburettor/diesel pump linkages.
- [ ] Job 55. Adjust carburettor.
- [ ] Job 56. Check idle speed and mixture.
- [ ] Job 57. Check exhaust emission.
- [ ] Job 58. Check pipes and hoses.
- [ ] Job 59. Lubricate bonnet release.
- [ ] Job 73. Change air cleaner element and clean housing.
- [ ] Job 74. Check and adjust valve clearances.
- [ ] Job 75. NOT DIESEL, OR PETROL MODELS WITH CATALYST Check ignition timing.

- [ ] Job 77. Check vacuum hoses.
- [ ] Job 78. Check/renew crankcase emission hoses.
- [ ] Job 79. Clean oil filler cap.
- [ ] Job 80. DIESEL ENGINES ONLY Check air-pump belt.
- [ ] Job 81. Renew spark plugs.
- [ ] Job 82. DIESEL ENGINES ONLY Clean glow plugs.
- [ ] Job 83. Clean/protect battery terminals.
- [ ] Job 84. Check battery specific gravity.
- [ ] Job 85. Replace fuel filter.
- [ ] Job 86. Fault code readout.
- [ ] Job 87. Check tool kit and jack.
- [ ] Job 88. Check light unit seals.
- [ ] Job 89. Check door/tailgate seals.
- [ ] Job 90. Adjust headlight alignment.
- [ ] Job 91. Renew wiper blades.
- [ ] Job 92. Check soft-top and frame.
- [ ] Job 93. Check floors.
- [ ] Job 94. Renew batteries in car alarm sender.
- [ ] Job 95. Check wiring and terminals.
- [ ] Job 96. Clean radiator exterior.

- [ ] Job 109. Replace coolant and clean expansion tank.
- [ ] Job 110. Check/renew coolant expansion tank cap.
- [ ] Job 111. Renew drive belts.

Every 24,000 Miles - Around the Car

- [ ] Job 5. Check tyre pressures.
- [ ] Job 6. Check front lights and indicators.
- [ ] Job 7. Check side indicator repeaters.
- [ ] Job 8. Check rear lights.
- [ ] Job 9. Number plate lights.
- [ ] Job 10. Interior lights.
- [ ] Job 11. Check windscreen wipers.
- [ ] Job 12. Windscreen washers.
- [ ] Job 13. Check battery electrolyte level.
- [ ] Job 14. Check horn.

- [ ] Job 27. Check wheel bolts.
- [ ] Job 29. Check ABS warning light.
- [ ] Job 30. Check windscreen.
- [ ] Job 31. Check and lubricate aerial.
- [ ] Job 60. Check seat belts and mountings.
- [ ] Job 61. Check seat mountings.
- [ ] Job 62. Check fuel filler-cap seal.
- [ ] Job 63. Lubricate hinges, locks, check straps.
- [ ] Job 64. Check shock absorber action.
- [ ] Job 65. Check wheel alignment.

Every 24,000 Miles - Under the Car

- [ ] Job 15. Check tyre treads.
- [ ] Job 16. Check spare wheel.
- [ ] Job 17. Touch-up paintwork.
- [ ] Job 18. Valet interior.
- [ ] Job 19. Improve visibility.
- [ ] Job 32. Check exhaust system and mountings.
- [ ] Job 33. Check brake and fuel lines.
- [ ] Job 34. Check steering rack gaiters.
- [ ] Job 35. Check drive shaft gaiters.
- [ ] Job 36. Check underside of car for leaks.
- [ ] Job 37. Clean mud traps.
- [ ] Job 66. Check/renew front brake pads.
- [ ] Job 67. Check brake discs.
- [ ] Job 68. Check rear brake shoes.
- [ ] Job 69. Check/renew rear brake pads.
- [ ] Job 70. Check rear brake discs.
- [ ] Job 71. Check brake proportioning valve.
- [ ] Job 72. Check steering ball-joints.
- [ ] Job 97. Check wheel bearings.
- [ ] Job 98. Check steering and suspension.
- [ ] Job 99. Check steering rack mountings.
- [ ] Job 100. Check front suspension units.
- [ ] Job 101. Check front suspension bushes.
- [ ] Job 102. Check rear springs and shock absorbers.
- [ ] Job 103. Check rear suspension bushes.

Job 104. Check engine and gearbox mountings.

Job 105. Check/adjust/lubricate hand-brake cable.

Job 106. Check underside of body structure.

Job 107. Clear drainage holes.

Job 108. Renew brake fluid.

Every 24,000 Miles - Road Test

Job 38. Clean controls.

Job 39. Check instruments and controls.

Job 40. Check throttle action.

Job 41. Check clutch action.

Job 42. Road test: brakes and steering.

Job 43. Check C.V. joints for noise.

Job 44. Check automatic transmission fluid.

Date serviced:..

Carried out by: ....
Garage Stamp or signature:

Parts/Accessories purchased (date, parts, source) ....
....
....
....
....

EVERY 27,000 MILES - OR EVERY TWENTY SEVEN MONTHS, WHICHEVER COMES FIRST

All the Jobs at this Service Interval have been carried forward from earlier Service Intervals and are to be repeated at this service.

Every 27,000 Miles - The Engine Bay

Job 1. Engine oil level.

Job 2. Check coolant level.

Job 3. Brake fluid level.

Job 4. Check windscreen wash level.

Job 20. Check alternator drive belt.

Job 21. **DIESEL ENGINED MODELS ONLY** Check vacuum pump drive belt.

Job 22. **DIESEL ENGINES ONLY** Drain fuel filter.

Job 23. **DIESEL ENGINES ONLY** Renew diesel engine oil.

Job 24. Replace diesel engine oil filter.

Job 25. Check brake and fuel lines.

Job 26. Check air filter.

Every 27,000 Miles - Around the Car

First carry out all Jobs listed under earlier Service intervals as applicable.

Job 5. Check tyre pressures.

Job 6. Check front lights and indicators.

Job 7. Check side indicator repeaters.

Job 8. Check rear lights.

Job 9. Number plate lights.

Job 10. Interior lights.

Job 11. Check windscreen wipers.

Job 12. Windscreen washers.

Job 13. Check battery electrolyte level.

Job 14. Check horn.

Job 27. Check wheel bolts.

Job 28. Check handbrake adjustment.

Job 29. Check ABS warning light.

Job 30. Check windscreen.

Job 31. Check and lubricate aerial.

Every 27,000 Miles - Under the Car

First carry out all Jobs listed under earlier Service intervals as applicable.

Job 15. Check tyre treads.

Job 16. Check spare wheel.

Job 17. Touch-up paintwork.

Job 18. Valet interior.

Job 19. Improve visibility.

Job 32. Check exhaust system and mountings.

Job 33. Check brake and fuel lines.

Job 34. Check steering rack gaiters.

Job 35. Check drive shaft gaiters.

Job 36. Check underside of car for leaks.

Job 37. Clean mud traps.

Every 27,000 Miles - Road Test

- [ ] Job 38. Clean controls.
- [ ] Job 39. Check instruments and controls.
- [ ] Job 40. Check throttle action.
- [ ] Job 41. Check clutch action.
- [ ] Job 42. Road test: brakes and steering.
- [ ] Job 43. Check C.V. joints for noise.
- [ ] Job 44. Check automatic transmission fluid.

EVERY 30,000 MILES - OR EVERY THIRTY MONTHS, WHICHEVER COMES FIRST

All the Jobs at this Service Interval have been carried forward from earlier Service Intervals and are to be repeated at this service.

Every 30,000 Miles - The Engine Bay

- [ ] Job 2. Check coolant level.
- [ ] Job 3. Brake fluid level.
- [ ] Job 4. Check windscreen wash level.
- [ ] Job 20. Check alternator drive belt.
- [ ] Job 21. **DIESEL ENGINED MODELS ONLY** Check vacuum pump drive belt.
- [ ] Job 22. **DIESEL ENGINES ONLY** Drain fuel filter.
- [ ] Job 23. **DIESEL ENGINES ONLY** Renew diesel engine oil.
- [ ] Job 24. Replace diesel engine oil filter.
- [ ] Job 25. Check brake and fuel lines.
- [ ] Job 45. Change engine oil and filter.
- [ ] Job 46. Clean and check spark plugs.
- [ ] Job 47. Clean and check ignition components.
- [ ] Job 48. Check water pump.
- [ ] Job 49. Lubricate/adjust clutch cable.
- [ ] Job 50. Check gearbox oil level.
- [ ] Job 51. Check power steering fluid level (where fitted).
- [ ] Job 52. Check and turn air cleaner element.
- [ ] Job 53. Lubricate throttle linkage.
- [ ] Job 54. Lubricate carburettor/diesel pump linkages.
- [ ] Job 55. Adjust carburettor.
- [ ] Job 56. Check idle speed and mixture.
- [ ] Job 57. Check exhaust emission.
- [ ] Job 58. Check pipes and hoses.
- [ ] Job 59. Lubricate bonnet release.

Every 30,000 Miles - Around the Car

- [ ] Job 5. Check tyre pressures.
- [ ] Job 6. Check front lights and indicators.
- [ ] Job 7. Check side indicator repeaters.
- [ ] Job 8. Check rear lights.
- [ ] Job 9. Number plate lights.
- [ ] Job 10. Interior lights.
- [ ] Job 11. Check windscreen wipers.
- [ ] Job 12. Windscreen washers.
- [ ] Job 13. Check battery electrolyte level.
- [ ] Job 14. Check horn.
- [ ] Job 27. Check wheel bolts.
- [ ] Job 29. Check ABS warning light.
- [ ] Job 30. Check windscreen.
- [ ] Job 31. Check and lubricate aerial.
- [ ] Job 60. Check seat belts and mountings.
- [ ] Job 61. Check seat mountings.
- [ ] Job 62. Check fuel filler-cap seal.
- [ ] Job 63. Lubricate hinges, locks, check straps.
- [ ] Job 64. Check shock absorber action.
- [ ] Job 65. Check wheel alignment.

Every 30,000 Miles - Under the Car

First carry out all Jobs listed under earlier Service intervals as applicable.

- [ ] Job 15. Check tyre treads.
- [ ] Job 16. Check spare wheel.
- [ ] Job 17. Touch-up paintwork.
- [ ] Job 18. Valet interior.
- [ ] Job 19. Improve visibility.
- [ ] Job 32. Check exhaust system and mountings.
- [ ] Job 33. Check brake and fuel lines.
- [ ] Job 34. Check steering rack gaiters.
- [ ] Job 35. Check drive shaft gaiters.
- [ ] Job 36. Check underside of car for leaks.
- [ ] Job 37. Clean mud traps.
- [ ] Job 66. Check/renew front brake pads.
- [ ] Job 67. Check brake discs.
- [ ] Job 68. Check rear brake shoes.

Date serviced:..

Carried out by:..
Garage Stamp or signature:

Parts/Accessories purchased (date, parts, source) ....

....

....

....

....

☐ Job 69. Check/renew rear brake pads.

☐ Job 70. Check rear brake discs.

☐ Job 71. Check brake proportioning valve.

☐ Job 72. Check steering ball-joints.

Every 30,000 Miles - Road Test

☐ Job 38. Clean controls.

☐ Job 39. Check instruments and controls.

☐ Job 40. Check throttle action.

☐ Job 41. Check clutch action.

☐ Job 42. Road test: brakes and steering.

☐ Job 43. Check C.V. joints for noise.

☐ Job 44. Check automatic transmission fluid.

EVERY 33,000 MILES - OR EVERY THIRTY THREE MONTHS, WHICHEVER COMES FIRST

All the Jobs at this Service Interval have been carried forward from earlier Service Intervals and are to be repeated at this service.

Every 33,000 Miles - The Engine Bay

☐ Job 1. Engine oil level.

☐ Job 2. Check coolant level.

☐ Job 3. Brake fluid level.

☐ Job 4. Check windscreen wash level.

☐ Job 20. Check alternator drive belt.

☐ Job 21. **DIESEL ENGINED MODELS ONLY** Check vacuum pump drive belt.

☐ Job 22. **DIESEL ENGINES ONLY** Drain fuel filter.

☐ Job 23. **DIESEL ENGINES ONLY** Renew diesel engine oil.

☐ Job 24. Replace diesel engine oil filter.

☐ Job 25. Check brake and fuel lines.

☐ Job 26. Check air filter.

Every 33,000 Miles - Around The Car

First carry out all Jobs listed under earlier Service intervals as applicable.

☐ Job 5. Check tyre pressures.

☐ Job 6. Check front lights and indicators.

☐ Job 7. Check side indicator repeaters.

☐ Job 8. Check rear lights.

☐ Job 9. Number plate lights.

☐ Job 10. Interior lights.

☐ Job 11. Check windscreen wipers.

☐ Job 12. Windscreen washers.

☐ Job 13. Check battery electrolyte level.

☐ Job 14. Check horn.

☐ Job 27. Check wheel bolts.

☐ Job 28. Check handbrake adjustment.

☐ Job 29. Check ABS warning light.

☐ Job 30. Check windscreen.

☐ Job 31. Check and lubricate aerial.

Every 33,000 Miles - Under the Car

First carry out all Jobs listed under earlier Service intervals as applicable.

☐ Job 15. Check tyre treads.

☐ Job 16. Check spare wheel.

☐ Job 17. Touch-up paintwork.

☐ Job 18. Valet interior.

☐ Job 19. Improve visibility.

☐ Job 32. Check exhaust system and mountings.

☐ Job 33. Check brake and fuel lines.

☐ Job 34. Check steering rack gaiters.

☐ Job 35. Check drive shaft gaiters.

☐ Job 36. Check underside of car for leaks.

☐ Job 37. Clean mud traps.

Date serviced:..

Carried out by:...
Garage Stamp or signature:

Parts/Accessories purchased (date, parts,

source)..
....
....
....
....

Every 33,000 Miles - Road Test

- [ ] Job 38. Clean controls.
- [ ] Job 39. Check instruments and controls.
- [ ] Job 40. Check throttle action.
- [ ] Job 41. Check clutch action.
- [ ] Job 42. Road test: brakes and steering.
- [ ] Job 43. Check C.V. joints for noise.
- [ ] Job 44. Check automatic transmission fluid.

Date serviced:..

Carried out by: ....
Garage Stamp or signature:

Parts/Accessories purchased (date, parts,

source) ....

....

....

....

....

EVERY 36,000 MILES - OR EVERY THREE YEARS, WHICHEVER COMES FIRST

All the Service Jobs in the tinted area have been carried forward from earlier service intervals and are to be repeated at this service.

Every 36,000 Miles - The Engine Bay

First carry out all Jobs listed under earlier Service intervals as applicable.

- [ ] Job 4. Check windscreen wash level.
- [ ] Job 20. Check alternator drive belt.
- [ ] Job 21. DIESEL ENGINED MODELS ONLY Check vacuum pump drive belt.
- [ ] Job 22. DIESEL ENGINES ONLY Drain fuel filter.
- [ ] Job 23. DIESEL ENGINES ONLY Renew diesel engine oil.
- [ ] Job 24. Replace diesel engine oil filter.
- [ ] Job 25. Check brake and fuel lines.
- [ ] Job 45. Change engine oil and filter.
- [ ] Job 47. Clean and check ignition components.
- [ ] Job 48. Check water pump.
- [ ] Job 49. Lubricate/adjust clutch cable.
- [ ] Job 50. Check gearbox oil level.
- [ ] Job 51. Check power steering fluid level (where fitted).
- [ ] Job 52. Check and turn air cleaner element.
- [ ] Job 53. Lubricate throttle linkage.
- [ ] Job 54. Lubricate carburettor/diesel pump linkages.
- [ ] Job 55. Adjust carburettor.
- [ ] Job 56. Check idle speed and mixture.
- [ ] Job 57. Check exhaust emission.
- [ ] Job 58. Check pipes and hoses.
- [ ] Job 59. Lubricate bonnet release.
- [ ] Job 73. Change air cleaner element and clean housing.
- [ ] Job 74. Check and adjust valve clearances.
- [ ] Job 75. NOT DIESEL, OR PETROL MODELS WITH CATALYST Check ignition timing.

- [ ] Job 77. Check vacuum hoses.
- [ ] Job 78. Check/renew crankcase emission hoses.
- [ ] Job 79. Clean oil filler cap.
- [ ] Job 80. DIESEL ENGINES ONLY Check air-pump belt.
- [ ] Job 81. Renew spark plugs.
- [ ] Job 82. DIESEL ENGINES ONLY Clean glow plugs.
- [ ] Job 83. Clean/protect battery terminals.
- [ ] Job 84. Check battery specific gravity.
- [ ] Job 85. Replace fuel filter.
- [ ] Job 86. Fault code readout.
- [ ] Job 87. Check tool kit and jack.
- [ ] Job 88. Check light unit seals.
- [ ] Job 89. Check door/tailgate seals.
- [ ] Job 90. Adjust headlight alignment.
- [ ] Job 91. Renew wiper blades.
- [ ] Job 92. Check soft-top and frame.
- [ ] Job 93. Check floors.
- [ ] Job 94. Renew batteries in car alarm sender.
- [ ] Job 95. Check wiring and terminals.
- [ ] Job 96. Clean radiator exterior.

- [ ] Job 112. Change gearbox oil/transmission fluid.
- [ ] Job 113. Renew camshaft belt.

Every 36,000 Miles - Around the Car

- [ ] Job 5. Check tyre pressures.
- [ ] Job 6. Check front lights and indicators.
- [ ] Job 7. Check side indicator repeaters.
- [ ] Job 8. Check rear lights.
- [ ] Job 9. Number plate lights.
- [ ] Job 10. Interior lights.
- [ ] Job 11. Check windscreen wipers.
- [ ] Job 12. Windscreen washers.
- [ ] Job 13. Check battery electrolyte level.
- [ ] Job 14. Check horn.

- ☐ Job 27. Check wheel bolts.
- ☐ Job 29. Check ABS warning light.
- ☐ Job 30. Check windscreen.
- ☐ Job 31. Check and lubricate aerial.
- ☐ Job 60. Check seat belts and mountings.
- ☐ Job 61. Check seat mountings.
- ☐ Job 62. Check fuel filler-cap seal.
- ☐ Job 63. Lubricate hinges, locks, check straps.
- ☐ Job 64. Check shock absorber action.
- ☐ Job 65. Check wheel alignment.

Every 36,000 Miles - Under the Car

- ☐ Job 15. Check tyre treads.
- ☐ Job 16. Check spare wheel.
- ☐ Job 17. Touch-up paintwork.
- ☐ Job 18. Valet interior.
- ☐ Job 19. Improve visibility.
- ☐ Job 32. Check exhaust system and mountings.
- ☐ Job 33. Check brake and fuel lines.
- ☐ Job 34. Check steering rack gaiters.
- ☐ Job 35. Check drive shaft gaiters.
- ☐ Job 36. Check underside of car for leaks.
- ☐ Job 37. Clean mud traps.
- ☐ Job 66. Check/renew front brake pads.
- ☐ Job 67. Check brake discs.
- ☐ Job 68. Check rear brake shoes.
- ☐ Job 69. Check/renew rear brake pads.
- ☐ Job 70. Check rear brake discs.
- ☐ Job 71. Check brake proportioning valve.
- ☐ Job 72. Check steering ball-joints.
- ☐ Job 97. Check wheel bearings.
- ☐ Job 98. Check steering and suspension.
- ☐ Job 99. Check steering rack mountings.
- ☐ Job 100. Check front suspension units.
- ☐ Job 101. Check front suspension bushes.
- ☐ Job 102. Check rear springs and shock absorbers.
- ☐ Job 103. Check rear suspension bushes.

- ☐ Job 104. Check engine and gearbox mountings.
- ☐ Job 105. Check/adjust/lubricate hand-brake cable.
- ☐ Job 106. Check underside of body structure.
- ☐ Job 107. Clear drainage holes.
- ☐ Job 108. Renew brake fluid.

☐ Job 114. Top-up rustproofing.

Every 36,000 Miles - Road Test

- ☐ Job 38. Clean controls.
- ☐ Job 39. Check instruments and controls.
- ☐ Job 40. Check throttle action.
- ☐ Job 41. Check clutch action.
- ☐ Job 42. Road test: brakes and steering.
- ☐ Job 43. Check C.V. joints for noise.
- ☐ Job 44. Check automatic transmission fluid.

LONGER TERM SERVICING

48,000 MILES - OR EVERY FOUR YEARS, WHICHEVER COMES FIRST

☐ Job 115. Renew HT leads, distributor cap and rotor arm.

72,000 MILES - OR EVERY SIX YEARS, WHICHEVER COMES FIRST

☐ Job 116. Renew glow plugs.

☐ Job 117. **FUEL INJECTION PETROL AND DIESEL ENGINES** Check and renew fuel injectors.

Date serviced:...

Carried out by:...
Garage Stamp or signature:

Parts/Accessories purchased (date, parts,
source) ....
....
....
....
....

Date serviced:...

Carried out by:...
Garage Stamp or signature:

Parts/Accessories purchased (date, parts,
source) ....
....
....
....
....

SERVICE HISTORY NOTES